ISBN 978-0-282-28183-0
PIBN 10564985

BULLETIN 198
California Division of Mines and Geology
Sacramento, California, 1973

urban geology

master plan for CALIFORNIA

GEOLOGIC HAZARDS IN CALIFORNIA
A $55 BILLION PROBLEM

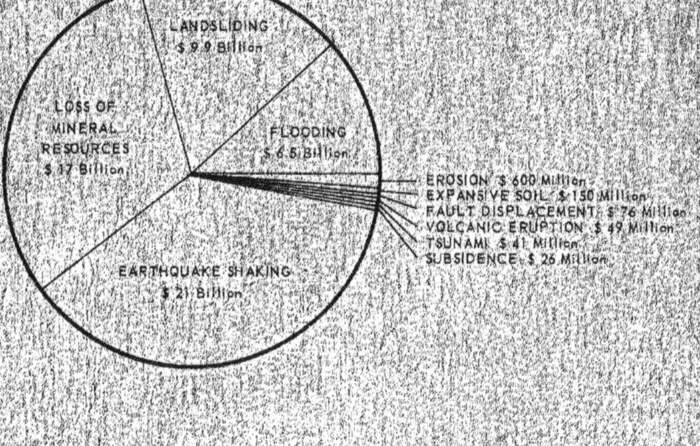

1973

urban geology

master plan for

CALIFORNIA

THE NATURE, MAONITUDE, AND COSTS OF GEOLOGIC HAZARDS IN CALIFORNIA AND RECOMMENDATIONS FOR THEIR MITIGATION.

PREPARED UNDER THE DIRECTION OF
WESLEY G. BRUER, STATE GEOLOGIST
by
John T. Alfors
John L. Burnett
Thomas E. Gay, Jr.

STATE OF C

RONALD REAG

DEPARTMENT OF

RAY B. HUNTE

PREPARED BY THE CALIF
IN COOPERATION WITH THE

STATE OF CALIFORNIA

RONALD REAGAN, *GOVERNOR*

THE RESOURCES AGENCY

NORMAN B. LIVERMORE, JR., *SECRETARY*

DEPARTMENT OF CONSERVATION

RAY B. HUNTER, *DIRECTOR*

DIVISION OF MINES AND GEOLOGY

WESLEY G. BRUER, *STATE GEOLOGIST*

The preparation of this report was financed in part through a comprehensive planning grant from the Department of Housing and Urban Development, under the provisions of Section 701 of the Housing Act of 1968, as amended.

PREPARED BY THE CALIFORNIA DIVISION OF MINES AND GEOLOGY, WESLEY G. BRUER, State Geologist
IN COOPERATION WITH THE OFFICE OF PLANNING AND RESEARCH, JOHN S. TOOKER, Director

CONTENTS

CONTENTS—Continued

ILLUSTRATIONS

ILLUSTRATIONS—Continued

ABSTRACT

The results of a three-year study of geologic problems in California are presented. The total projected loss attributable to property damage, life loss and loss of mineral resources, including both direct and indirect costs, caused by ten geologic problems in California from 1970 to 2000 is estimated to be $55 billion. Four problems—earthquake shaking, loss of mineral resources, landsliding, and flooding—account for 98 percent of the total projected loss. The remaining 2 percent of the estimated loss is due to erosion activity, expansive soils, fault displacement, volcanic hazards, tsunami hazards, and subsidence.

The state of the art relative to measures to reduce losses caused by the ten geologic problems is reviewed and benefit:cost ratios are presented for each problem. An estimated $38 billion of the $55 billion total projected loss could be prevented by application of current state-of-the-art loss-reduction measures. The total cost of applying these measures is estimated at $6 billion, for an overall benefit:cost ratio of 6.2:1. In addition, then, to satisfying the needs for increased public safety and the social and political concerns therefor, geologic hazards loss-reduction is also "good business."

The degree of effectiveness of the various types of loss-reduction measures possible are reviewed and recommendations are presented. The most effective action that can be taken is for cities and counties to strengthen and diligently enforce existing grading ordinances and building codes.

A methodology for setting priorities for the application of loss-reduction measures is presented. The study concludes that no single ranking of priorities with respect to localities, specific problems, or particular loss-reduction programs, is feasible; but the actions taken should commence in the more populated and the more hazardous areas.

Section 1

Summary of Findings Conclusions and Recommendations

SUMMARY OF FINDINGS, CONCLUSIONS, AND RECOMMENDATIONS

General Summary

With the vigorous and widespread application of loss-reduction measures, most of which are economically attractive, the majority of the geologic losses projected below can be avoided or prevented. Otherwise, given a continuation of present practices, it is estimated that property damage and the dollar equivalent of life loss directly attributable to geologic processes and conditions and the loss of mineral resources due to urbanization will amount to more than $55 billion in California between 1970 and the year 2000 (table 1, column 2). This loss compares closely with the estimated total loss of $50 billion * due to urban and wildland fires in the state during the same period. The relative losses attributable to the ten geologic problems considered in this report, in order of decreasing percentage of the total $55 billion projected loss, are:

Geologic problems	*Percent of total loss*
Earthquake shaking	38
Loss of mineral resources	30
Landsliding	18
Flooding	12
Erosion activity	1
Expansive soils	0.3
Fault displacement	0.15
Volcanic hazards	0.1
Tsunami hazards	0.1
Subsidence	0.05

The relative percentage losses are shown graphically in figure 1 and the dollar values are given in table 1, column 2.

The recommendations for reducing losses from geologic problems fall into two major categories: (1) those that propose to improve the state of the art by developing new capabilities, and (2) those that propose to extend the application of present state-of-the-art procedures. In general, a sequence of steps is required for any effective action program to reduce losses due to geologic problems. First, the nature, extent, and severity of the problem must be recognized. Second, solutions for the problem need to be devised where possible. Third, contingency plans and preparations need to be made for responding to those problems that cannot be solved adequately. Fourth, long-range recovery actions should be planned for the catastrophic problems. Often the key to whether loss-reduction measures are adequately implemented is the degree of enforcement provided by local government. Some of the problems, such as expansive soils, tsunami hazards, landsliding, and loss of mineral resources, can be solved to a large extent by the application of current state-of-the-art procedures. All that is needed is the requirement that appropriate known loss-reduction measures be applied and that the requirement be effectively enforced. Effective mitigation of the other problems requires various degrees of improvement in the state of the art.

If current practices were upgraded to the current state of the art and all presently feasible loss-reduction measures were applied throughout California, an estimated $38 billion reduction in projected losses could be realized. The total cost of applying the loss-reduction measures is estimated to be $6 billion, and the overall benefit:cost ratio 6.2:1. The estimated benefits, costs, and benefit:cost ratios for each of the ten geologic problems are given in table 1; figure 2 presents similar data graphically.

In order to effect greater loss reduction, remedies other than those currently known and being applied would have to be devised and used. For example, breakthroughs in earthquake prediction and earthquake control could result in large reductions of projected losses due to earthquake shaking. Increased research by universities, governmental agencies, and private firms, therefore, is indicated. The benefit:cost ratios for loss-reduction by new or additional types of research are difficult to predict, but the potential for loss-reductions is enormous, and the possibilities, therefore, for large benefit:cost ratios are equally great.

Losses can be reduced even further by vigorous enforcement of improved building codes that result in greater earthquake-resistant design of structures. The application of improved building codes, if begun in the design stage, generally adds only a few percent (typically 1 to 2 percent) to the total cost of the structures. Benefit:cost ratios relative to the enforcement of improved building codes are difficult to assess because of the many variables involved. However, the benefit:cost ratios that apply to the reduction of structural damage are likely to be relatively low because, although the increased costs would apply to every new structure, relatively few buildings would be subject to extensive damage during their useful life.

For existing hazardous structures, the cost of remedial work generally will amount to a relatively large percentage of the total value of a structure, and the benefit:cost ratio, therefore, may be relatively small when considering property damage alone. However, the improvement work would result in substantial reduction to the threat of life loss and the social value alone should warrant carrying out such measures. The demolition of some hazardous buildings may be justified economically as well as socially, depending on the value placed on human life. Similarly, the strengthening or removal of hazardous parapets and appendages is almost always justifiable. An additional incentive is to reduce the possibility of law suits

* The fire loss figure has been extrapolated based on a value of $16 billion per year national loss from major structural fires and $7.5 million per year average fire loss to state responsibility wildlands in California.

*Table 1. Projected losses due to geologic problems in California, 1970–2000 (estimated)**

(Column 1)	(Column 2)	(Column 3)		(Column 4)		(Column 5)
	Projected total losses, 1970–2000, without improvement of existing policies and practices	*Possible total loss reduction 1970–2000, applying all feasible measures*		*Estimated total cost of applying all feasible measures, at current state of the art, 1970–2000*		*Benefit: Cost ratio if all feasible measures were applied and all possible loss reductions were achieved, 1970–2000*
Geologic problem		*Percent of total loss*	*Dollar amount*	*Percent of total loss*	*Dollar amount*	
Earthquake shaking	$21,035,000,000	50**	$10,517,500,000	10	$2,103,500,000	5
Loss of mineral resources	17,000,000,000	90	15,000,000,000	0.53	90,000,000	167
Landsliding	9,850,000,000	90	8,865,000,000	10.3	1,018,000,000	8.7
Flooding	6,532,000,000	52.5	3,432,000,000	41.4	2,703,000,000	1.3
Erosion activity	565,000,000	66	377,000,000	45.7	250,000,000	1.5
Expansive soils	150,000,000	99	148,500,000	5	7,500,000	20
Fault displacement	76,000,000	17	12,600,000	10	7,500,000	1.7
Volcanic hazards	49,380,000	16.5	8,135,000	3.5	1,655,000	4.9
Tsunami hazards	40,800,000	95	37,760,000	63	25,700,000	1.5
Subsidence	26,400,000	50	13,200,000	65.1	8,790,000	1.5
TOTALS	$55,324,580,000	69	$38,411,695,000	11.2	$6,215,645,000	6.2

* See Appendix for explanation of the derivation of the data in this table.
** 90 percent reduction of life loss.

Column 2: Estimated total dollar loss, 1970 to 2000 for all of California; about 95 percent of the loss would be in urban areas. These values are based on the assumptions that the number and severity of each type of event occurs as estimated, and that no change is made in the 1970 type, effectiveness, or level of application of preventive and remedial measures.

Column 3: Estimated total loss-reduction in dollars and in percent of projected loss, for all of California, assuming an aggressive but reasonable degree of improvement in the 1970 type and level of preventive and remedial measures. Conservative improvements in the state of the art, application over wider area, and more effective application and follow-up of all known types of loss-reduction measures over the next 30 years are assumed.

Column 4: Estimated total cost of applying loss-reduction measures of the type, effectiveness, and extent visualized in column 3, for all of California, for the period 1970–2000 in dollars and in percent of projected total loss (column 4 : column 2).

Column 5: Estimated benefit : cost ratio (column 3 : column 4) based on the estimated cost (column 4) of applying the estimated loss-reduction measures to obtain the estimated reductions (column 3) of the estimated total losses (column 2).

Data in table 1 were collected from the analyses of losses and loss-reduction costs for individual problems in Section 7, Appendix A, "Costs of Losses and Loss-Reduction Measures". All figures are 1970 dollars.

leveled against local governments in the event of subsequent damage (see Sheffer decision, Section 7, Appendix C). The courts are beginning to consider the liability of those responsible for the planning, design, construction, and permit approval where disasters have occurred rather than treating such catastrophes as "acts of God" (Hughes, 1971, p. 72).

Land-use zoning can be a particularly effective loss-reduction measure, yet is not fully used at present, partly because of concern for possible inverse condemnation lawsuits. Nonetheless, if any doubt exists as to the safety of a proposed development, construction permits should not be issued or issued only after such doubts have been investigated and removed. Public safety should be the primary concern.

The addition of geologists to the staffs of planning, engineering, building and safety, and/or public works departments of counties and the larger cities for plan review and on-site inspection of geologic conditions is recommended as an effective loss-reduction measure.

As demonstrated by many jurisdictions in California, the single most effective action that can be taken to reduce losses due to geologic problems is for cities and counties to adopt and diligently enforce modern grading ordinances and building codes.

Foreseeable advances in the state-of-the-art of loss-reduction measures potentially could result in near-zero life loss due to geologic hazards. Property damage could ultimately be reduced by as much as 90 percent.

The magnitude of the geologic hazards problem in California and the degree to which it is being resolved should be subject to periodic review. It is recommended that an annual status report be prepared by an appropriate state agency or agencies. The Governor's Earthquake Council, the Legislature's Joint Committee on Seismic Safety, or successor groups would

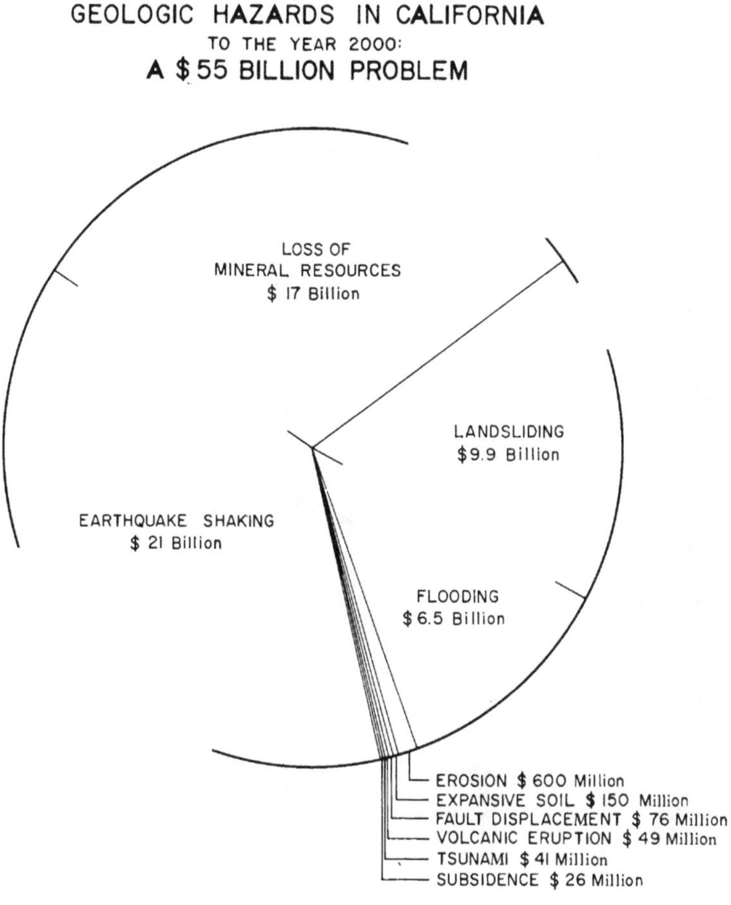

Figure 1. Geologic hazards in California to the year 2000: a $55 billion problem. Estimated magnitude of losses due to ten geologic problems in California projected from 1970 to the year 2000, if current loss-reduction practices continue unchanged.

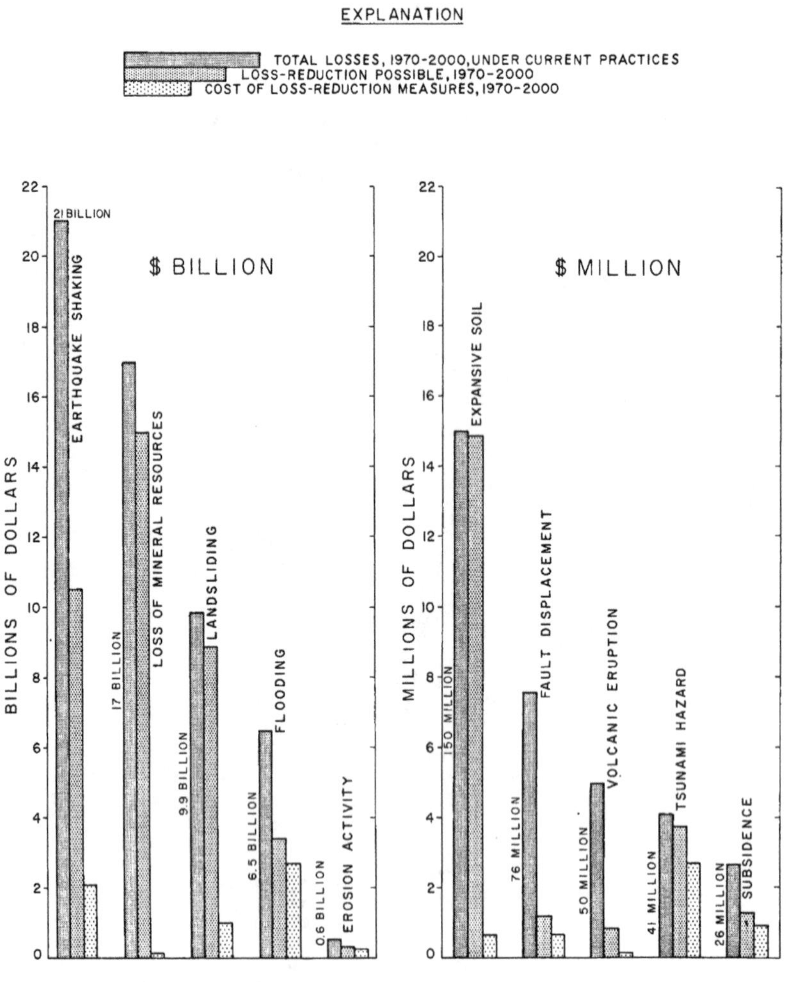

Figure 2. Estimated total losses due to each of ten geologic problems in California for the period 1970–2000, under current practices; amount of loss-reduction possible, if state-of-the-art practices were used; and cost of applying state-of-the-art loss-reduction practices.

be appropriate bodies to evaluate such reviews.

Although not strictly a loss-reduction measure, insurance programs can provide an element of protection to property owners. Consideration should be given to the establishment of a broad-coverage, natural-disaster insurance program to include geologic hazards. Such a program could parallel that already initiated by the Federal Department of Housing and Urban Development with respect to flood and mudslide insurance.

Earthquake Shaking

A. FINDINGS

Given a continuation of present conditions, it is estimated that losses due to earthquake shaking will total $21 billion in California between 1970 and the year 2000. Most of the damage and loss of life will occur in zones of known high seismic activity; structures that do not comply with the provisions of the Field and Riley Acts, passed in 1933, will be especially vulnerable.

Losses from earthquake shaking will be greater than those from any other geologic problem. As many as 10,360 deaths and 40,360 hospitalized injuries have been projected to result from an 8.3 magnitude earthquake on the San Andreas fault near San Francisco (Algermissen *et al.*, 1972, p. 121). An estimated 30,000 probable deaths would result from earthquake-induced dam failures in the San Francisco Bay Area (Algermissen *et al.*, 1972, p. 132). A hypothetical, but expectable, large earthquake in the Los Angeles area has been projected to result in 10,000 deaths (Duke, 1971). If present-day techniques for reducing losses from earthquake shaking were applied to the fullest degree, life loss could be reduced by at least 90 percent, and the total dollar value of losses could be reduced by as much as 50 percent. Total costs for performing the loss-reduction work would be about 10 percent of the total projected loss, which with 50 percent effectiveness provides a benefit:cost ratio of 5:1.

The greatest threat to life and property is posed by those structures that do not conform to the current Uniform Building Code relative to earthquake loading. Applying loss-reduction measures to these structures is a major challenge because of the political, social, and economic problems involved. Great benefit would be achieved in preventing life loss, but the benefit:cost ratio to prevent property damage would be relatively low. Partial reduction of the structural hazards such as strengthening or removing parapets and cornices and reducing occupancy exposure by a lesser intensity of use will have higher benefit:cost ratios.

A generally higher benefit:cost ratio can be achieved by applying loss-reduction efforts to areas undergoing rapid urbanization rather than to areas already developed. The urbanizing areas are largely on the margins of the Los Angeles metropolitan area and to lesser extents the southern San Francisco Bay Area near San Jose and the vicinity of San Diego.

An effective earthquake prediction or warning system could save numerous lives both in existing urban areas and in rapidly urbanizing areas. With current and projected levels of funding, it is possible that an effective prediction system may be devised in 5 to 10 years. An effective earthquake control mechanism would result in tremendous reduction in property damage as well as life loss, but such a system does not appear feasible in the foreseeable future.

B. CONCLUSIONS

Losses, especially life loss, due to shaking from future earthquakes can and should be reduced through a combination of measures involving geologic and seismologic research, engineering practice, building codes, urban planning and zoning, fiscal and taxation policy, and preparedness planning. Close coordination is needed between local, state, and federal agencies, universities, and the private sector, to accomplish the goal without duplication of effort.

Priority efforts, such as strengthening, demolishing, or reducing to a lesser use, need to be applied to reducing life loss due to collapse of hazardous old buildings.

Priority for geologic and seismologic efforts should be given to areas which are undergoing redevelopment or rapid urbanization or which are anticipated to become urbanized between the present and the year 2000.

Enactment of controls, and parapet ordinances must be implemented by providing funds and personnel for vigorous enforcement. Although the Uniform Building Code is designed to be a model for minimum acceptable standards, some designers and builders use it as a maximum. The Uniform Building Code, 1970 edition, should be upgraded relative to earthquake shaking forces.

C. RECOMMENDATIONS

Recommendations for earthquake loss-reduction measures are presented in detail in the *First Report of the Governor's Earthquake Council*, November 1972, available through the California Division of Mines and Geology at cost; further recommendations will develop as a result of continuing work by the Council pursuant to the implementation sections of those recommendations.

In addition, the forthcoming final report of the Joint Committee on Seismic Safety of the California Legislature will also contain recommendations, both complementary and supplementary to those of the Governor's Earthquake Council. Therefore, detailed recommendations relative to loss-reduction measures for earthquake shaking are not repeated here.

Loss of Mineral Resources

A. FINDINGS

Loss of mineral resources due to urbanization between 1970 and the year 2000 is estimated to total $17 billion if current practices are continued. The mineral resources under greatest urbanization pressure are the construction materials, especially sand and gravel and crushed stone. The estimated losses are based largely on the added cost to the public due to increased transportation costs, the cost of relocating mining operations farther from markets, and the use of lower grade deposits that require more processing. Some mineral deposits being threatened by urbanization are unique and cannot be replaced. The environmental costs of mining deposits farther from markets, such as more vehicles required, more fuel used, and resultant increased air pollution, and increased road maintenance, are not included in the cost figures herein.

The per capita demand for construction materials has increased in the past and is expected to continue to increase in the future. Therefore, even more construction materials than are currently used per year will be required in the future despite lowered population growth expectations.

B. CONCLUSIONS

Mining operations required to supply urban needs should be located as close to markets as suitable deposits permit, and appropriate land use designations should be provided. Unique mineral deposits, especially, should be protected from urbanization.

C. RECOMMENDATIONS

The California Division of Mines and Geology, the U.S. Geological Survey, and the U.S. Bureau of Mines should intensify their efforts to catalog those mineral resources of critical importance to the future economy of California that are within and adjacent to urban areas.

Mineral deposits of economic size and quality constitute only a small fraction of one percent of the earth's crust, making them one of the rarest (and most valuable) environments of all. Therefore, local governments should protect the critical mineral resources, access thereto, and the mining thereof within their jurisdictions by special zoning, with buffer zones around them as necessary. In turn, mine operators should be required to conduct operations as compatibly as practicable with their surroundings and should be expected to rehabilitate depleted mined-lands for subsequent beneficial use such as parks, open space, or urban development.

Demand projections should be made for the critical mineral commodities used in California. Local governments should be aware of their future mineral resource requirements to plan better for the use of the deposits available to them.

Landsliding

A. FINDINGS

Under present conditions, it is estimated that losses due to landsliding will total almost $10 billion in California between 1970 and the year 2000. Loss of life is not expected to be great. Most of the damage will occur in the hillside areas of western California that are underlain by Cenozoic and Mesozoic sedimentary rocks. The severity of the problem depends upon the local bedrock and soil conditions, including moisture content, vegetation, slope, and other factors.

Although landslides and landslide-prone areas can be identified with about 90 percent accuracy by geologic studies, only a small portion of the area subject to landslide damage has been mapped in sufficient detail for local government land-use planning. Many local governments thus are not fully aware of the potential landslide hazards within their jurisdictions.

Grading ordinances have been adopted by most local governments; many are based on Chapter 70 of the Uniform Building Code, 1970 edition. Although the grading ordinances may be adequate, often they are not adequately implemented for lack of trained personnel and thus are less effective than they could be. The benefit:cost ratio for an effectively enforced grading ordinance is estimated to be about 9:1.

B. CONCLUSIONS

Losses due to landsliding can be reduced by 90 percent or more by a combination of measures involving geologic investigations, engineering practice, and effective enforcement of grading ordinances. The Los Angeles City grading ordinance and enforcement procedures have resulted in effective control of almost 99 percent of the potential landslides in their jurisdiction. A less elaborate system could reduce 90 percent of the losses in California at a relatively low cost.

C. RECOMMENDATIONS

Geologic mapping, at scales ranging from 1:12,000 to 1:48,000, should be carried out in all areas subject to urban development, on a priority basis, to identify landslides and landslide-prone areas. Cities and counties should be responsible to see that this is done within their jurisdictions prior to approval of general development patterns. The geologic mapping can be done by private consultants, by local government staff, or in cooperation with the California Division of Mines and Geology.

Detailed engineering geology site studies should be required for proposed developments within landslide and landslide-prone areas, prior to designing each development. These studies should be carried out by private consultants hired by the developers.

Proposed developments within landslide and landslide-prone areas should be engineered to avoid or correct all slope stability problems found by the detailed engineering geology studies.

Geologic and engineering reports should be reviewed for adequacy by qualified professionals, and qualified local government grading inspectors should inspect various stages of the development to insure that all work necessary to prevent future landslide problems is being done.

Local government should enforce adequate grading ordinances (Chapter 70, Uniform Building Code) by on-site inspection of developments in landslide and landslide-prone areas by qualified grading inspectors. Certification should be required by design civil engineers, soils engineers, and engineering geologists.

Flooding

A. FINDINGS

It is estimated that losses due to flooding will total more than $6.5 billion between 1970 and the year 2000 if the present level of flood-control measures is maintained. More than half of the estimated losses could be prevented by the prompt application of all economically feasible control measures. The cost of the control measures would be slightly less than the estimated cost of the flood damage. Flood control measures that can be taken include:

(1) construction and adequate maintenance of engineering works, such as dams, levees, unobstructed by-pass and overflow systems, and flood-control basins,

(2) implementation of flood warning systems,

(3) preparation of adequate evacuation plans for all areas subject to flooding by 100-year floods or by dam failure, and

(4) adoption of flood plain zoning ordinances and regulations to control the type of structures permitted in high-risk areas, and requiring that structures permitted in high-risk areas are built in such a way as to minimize flood losses.

B. CONCLUSIONS

Most of the flood damage to urban areas takes place because flood plains provide much of the habitable area of the state. Development in these areas is often not regulated adequately to cope with runoff from infrequent intense storms in California. Natural drainage channels are filled, narrowed, or allowed to become obstructed to the extent that they no longer accommodate even minor floods. The past federal and State policy of providing disaster relief to cover flood damage without any limitations on rebuilding has not discouraged the practice of building in flood-prone areas. The recent National Flood Insurance Program of the Federal Department of Housing and Urban Development is a step in the right direction, in that flood insurance payments will be made only once, and structures are not to be rebuilt in recognized flood-prone areas.

C. RECOMMENDATIONS

Flood control projects such as those constructed by the Army Corps of Engineers in cooperation with local flood control districts should be encouraged where substantial benefit accrues to the public. Costs of the projects should be borne in proportion to benefits to the beneficiaries.

All cities and counties in California should regulate construction in flood-prone areas through the adoption and diligent enforcement of realistic flood-plain zoning ordinances and building codes. Cities and counties should take the measures necessary to qualify for the National Flood Insurance Program of the Federal Department of Housing and Urban Development.

The Department of Water Resources and the National Weather Service should evaluate the need to expand the flood warning service in California in areas which are not adequately covered.

The California Department of Water Resources should coordinate studies by federal and State agencies in detailed delineation of flood-prone areas in California and development of flood-plain information for local agencies.

Erosion Activity

A. FINDINGS

It is estimated that losses due to erosion activity will total $565 million between 1970 and the year 2000 if current practices are continued unchanged. The losses due to erosion activity are difficult to separate from those due to flooding and landsliding. Within urban areas, the major costs of erosion activity are in removing sediment from public and private drainage systems.

Coastal erosion is a special problem involving wave action and is most severe during storms. Engineering works such as those constructed by the Army Corps of Engineers can reduce coastal erosion problems locally, but too often, as in the past, the problems may just be transferred to another site. Coastal erosion studies can provide a basis for avoiding development in areas subject to this problem.

B. CONCLUSIONS

About two-thirds of the projected losses due to erosion, siltation, and sedimentation in urban areas could be reduced by proper engineering design and construction practices. State codes and local regulations, such as grading ordinances, generally are adequate, but the main deficiency is lack of uniformly effective implementation. Losses due to coastal erosion can be reduced most economically by simply avoiding construction in areas subject to severe erosion.

C. RECOMMENDATIONS

All cities and counties should fully implement existing codes, ordinances, and regulations relative to grading (Chapter 70, Uniform Building Code), landscaping, and drainage by on-site inspection conducted by qualified engineers and geologists. This will reduce damage to property and protect cities and counties from law suits by citizens whose property otherwise might have been damaged.

Cities and counties in coastal areas should inventory areas subject to coastal erosion, determine erosion rates for each such area, and govern land use therein accordingly. These studies could be carried out in cooperation with the Army Corps of Engineers.

All construction projects designed to control coastal erosion should be carefully evaluated so that the correction of a problem in one area will not cause a problem in another. Similarly, prior to the construction of flood control facilities, the effect they have on coastal erosion by trapping sand and gravel that would otherwise be transported to beaches should be determined.

Expansive Soils

A. FINDINGS

It is estimated that losses in California due to expansive (shrink-swell) soils will total $150 million between 1970 and the year 2000 if present practices are continued. Expansive soils occur locally throughout California wherever relatively large percentages of clay minerals are present in the soil. The general distribution of expansive soils is well known in about one-third of the state through recent soil mapping by the Soil Conservation Service. Losses due to expansive soils can be eliminated completely if the condition is recognized before construction and foundations are properly engineered. Adequate controls exist for preventing damage due to expansive soils, both in State codes and local government regulations. Costs for corrective action before construction are small, but remedial action after construction may amount to 10 percent or more of the value of the structure.

B. CONCLUSIONS

The principal reason that newly built structures sustain damage attributable to expansive soils is that not all local governments apply existing codes and regulations effectively.

C. RECOMMENDATIONS

All cities and counties should insure effective enforcement of existing codes and regulations through inspection of site soil conditions and foundation designs by qualified soils and foundation engineers. This will reduce property damage and protect cities and counties from lawsuits by citizens whose property otherwise might have been damaged. Losses can be greatly reduced by full implementation of Chapter 70, Uniform Building Code, or more stringent grading ordinances.

Fault Displacement

A. FINDINGS

Losses from fault displacement are expected to be low compared to losses from earthquake shaking. It is estimated that between 1970 and the year 2000, under present conditions, fault displacement losses will reach a total of $76 million.

These losses will occur primarily along well-recognized faults in urban areas and at the margins of urban centers. However, past experience indicates that some active faults have not or cannot be recognized at the surface. Losses will result not only from displacement accompanying earthquakes, but also from fault creep, which displaces the ground along faults without violent earthquake shaking.

Very little can be done to provide protection for structures presently in place across active faults, short of moving the structures. Reduction of future losses can be accomplished best by careful selection of sites for construction. Careful investigation and selection of sites will result in re-siting, prior to construction, of an estimated 85 percent of the structures that otherwise would be built across active faults. When the cost of site evaluation is compared to the value of future structures saved by re-siting, a benefit to cost ratio of about 9.7:1 results.

B. CONCLUSIONS

The benefits from safeguarding future construction against fault displacement justify requiring detailed site investigations in and near seismically active zones. Zoning and inspection can assist in providing protection to the public against future losses by prohibiting the building of structures across active faults. Where structures, such as pipelines, aqueducts, and highways, must be built across active faults, they should be designed to accommodate the anticipated fault displacements and creep.

Insurance programs can provide an element of protection for owners of existing structures unknowingly built across active faults.

C. RECOMMENDATIONS

The identification and delineation of known and potentially active faults, as called for under the Alquist-Priolo Geologic Hazards Zones Act (Chapter 7.5, Division 2 of the California Public Resources Code), should continue to be carried out rapidly by the California Division of Mines and Geology.

Geologic site investigations should be required prior to consideration of approval for development in all seismically active areas, and construction setback requirements should be required by local governments along all identified active and potentially active faults.

Cities and counties should inventory existing structures across active faults. These structures should be removed or downgraded in level of use or occupancy, in accordance with some reasonable timetable.

Consideration should be given to legislation that will require lending institutions to require fault displacement insurance on residential properties as a condition to the granting of a loan on such properties. The fault displacement insurance could be included within a broad-coverage natural disaster insurance program. Insurance organizations should assure themselves that proposed structures are relatively free from potential fault displacement damage before insuring properties against such damages.

Volcanic Hazards

A. FINDINGS

Under present conditions, it is estimated that losses due to future volcanic eruptions could amount to $50 million between 1970 and the year 2000. Loss of life is not expected to be a large factor. Damage is most likely to occur in the vicinity of Mt. Shasta and Mt. Lassen and less likely at other Quaternary volcanic centers in California. General areas of potential hazard are known to geologists, but local government officials in the areas of concern may not be fully aware of the potential hazards.

Nothing can now be done to prevent and little to control volcanic eruptions. The most effective loss-reduction measure is to avoid vulnerable areas such as the natural drainage courses down slope from recently active volcanic areas. Major volcanic eruptions are generally preceded by smaller events that can be detected instrumentally and can serve as warnings of coming eruptions.

B. CONCLUSIONS

The major urban areas of California are relatively safe from the threat of volcanic eruptions. Warning systems can greatly reduce the threat of life loss from volcanic eruptions and land-use zoning can, to a limited extent, be used to prevent potential property damage.

C. RECOMMENDATIONS

The known recent volcanic centers in California should be instrumented or otherwise monitored to assure adequate warning prior to a volcanic eruption. This program should be conducted by the federal government, either through the U.S. Geological Survey or the National Oceanic and Atmospheric Administration; major potential volcanic threats are on federal lands.

Cities and counties in the areas of recent volcanism should evaluate the potential for damage to their jurisdictions and zone or regulate the development in these areas in accordance with the relative risks involved.

These jurisdictions should also consider the development of evacuation and other contingency plans.

Some of the younger volcanic cones and the nearby surrounding areas could be obtained for county or State parkland. This would preserve the geologic feature and provide protection to the public.

Tsunami Hazards

A. FINDINGS

It is estimated that losses due to tsunami damage will amount to about $40 million between 1970 and the year 2000. Most of the losses will occur in the coastal areas below the 20-foot elevation above mean low water level. The greatest damage can be expected in Crescent City, Del Norte County, but other sections of the California coast and offshore islands such as Santa Catalina are also subject to damage. Tsunamis cannot be prevented, but an effective warning system may give many hours of warning. If the warnings are heeded and proper action taken, life loss can be eliminated and property damage reduced. The National Oceanic and Atmospheric Administration currently administers a reasonably effective seismic sea-wave warning system.

B. CONCLUSIONS

An estimated 95 percent of all projected losses due to tsunamis can be prevented by a combination of coastal land-use zoning and an effective tsunami warning system.

C. RECOMMENDATIONS

The National Oceanic and Atmospheric Administration should be requested to prepare information on the expected tsunami runup along the California coast for 20,- 50,- and 100-year recurrence intervals.

Local governments should establish use zones along the coastline so that:

(1) no permanently inhabited structures other than those absolutely required be permitted within the 20-year recurrence runup zone,

(2) low intensity uses only be permitted within the 50-year recurrence runup zone,

(3) schools, hospitals, other critical facilities, and public buildings be located above the 100-year recurrence runup zone.

Subsidence

A. FINDINGS

It is estimated that losses due to subsidence will total over $26 million between 1970 and the year 2000 if current practices are continued. Most of the losses will be due to ground-water withdrawal and hydrocompaction. Subsidence due to oil and gas withdrawal can be and has been effectively controlled by water injection where monitoring and regulation are in effect. Areas subject to subsidence by ground-water withdrawal are well known and subsidence can be avoided by restricting ground-water withdrawal to the amount of recharge. Hydrocompaction occurs mainly in the more arid parts of California when man first applies large amounts of water. Control for hydrocompaction is expensive, but losses can be reduced if the condition is recognized and corrective action taken.

B. CONCLUSIONS

Subsidence due to oil and gas withdrawal is being controlled satisfactorily as regulated by the State Division of Oil and Gas. Subsidence due to ground-water withdrawal is being moderated by State and federal water projects by providing surface water supplies to areas which are experiencing lowering ground-water tables. Subsidence due to hydrocompaction has been studied by the State Department of Water Resources and the U.S. Geological Survey, but not all the areas subject to hydrocompaction have been identified.

C. RECOMMENDATIONS

The State Division of Oil and Gas should continue their subsidence monitoring and regulating program with respect to oil and gas withdrawals and repressuring and extend this program as needed to prevent damage to urban development. The program should be coordinated with local county or city engineers to assure that no adverse effects are occurring.

Ground-water withdrawal should be regulated where necessary to reduce subsidence, particularly in urban areas.

Cities and counties should make evaluations of the potential areas of damaging subsidence due to hydrocompaction within their jurisdictions and require corrective or preventive measures before approving permits for development of these lands. Geologic studies can determine if the potential for hydrocompaction exists. Detailed analyses of suspect areas should be made by a soils engineer.

Section 2

Introduction

Purpose and His

The Urban Geology M
ceived by the Department
a vehicle for State and
the needs of California
relative to geologic hazard
eral resources. The pro
Division of Mines and Ge
Conservation with the ass
and in cooperation with
Research of the Governor
in three phases over the three
1970, to June 30, 19 . P
was provided through
from the Department of H
ment under provisions
Act of 1968, as amended.

The project was desig
identification of present
ment-geologic environment
government and private se
mendations; program pr
ganizational needs. The
to serve as a basis for p
government, and by the
report is to be used as a gui
hazards and the conservat
areas of urban development
define and elucidate the m
or minimize life loss and p
areas due to dynamic geo
the loss of mineral reve
reduction measures having
cost ratios were determined.

Woodward-Lundgren
selected as the consultant
Leighton and Associates,
services for Phase II. No
quired for Phase III.

The primary objective
develop and apply a method
for geologic investigations
areas of California. Other
the best means of presenting
use by planners and engineers
with functions and capabilities
logic problems in California
II were to test the method
in five quarter quadrangles,
ogy as warranted, to determin
specific loss-reduction measure
urban geology master plan. P
view and revision of the draft
publication of the final pro
ogy for setting priorities
Phase I and modified in Phase
tion 5.

INTRODUCTION

Purpose and History of the Project

The Urban Geology Master Plan project was conceived by the Department of Conservation in 1969 as a vehicle for State and local government to respond to the needs of California for safe and orderly growth relative to geologic hazards and conservation of mineral resources. The project was conducted by the Division of Mines and Geology of the Department of Conservation with the assistance of private consultants and in cooperation with the Office of Planning and Research of the Governor's Office. It was carried out in three phases over the three-year period from July 1, 1970, to June 30, 1973. Partial funding for the project was provided through comprehensive planning grants from the Department of Housing and Urban Development under provisions of Section 701 of the Housing Act of 1968, as amended.

The project was designed to include the regional identification of present and potential urban development-geologic environment conflicts; a critique of government and private sector responsibilities; recommendations; program priorities; and legislative and organizational needs. The present final project report is to serve as a basis for policy making by State and local government, and by the private sector. In effect, the report is to be used as a guide for dealing with geologic hazards and the conservation of mineral resources in areas of urban development. The prime goal was to define and elucidate the measures necessary to avoid or minimize life loss and property damage in urban areas due to dynamic geologic processes and to reduce the loss of mineral resources to urbanization. Loss-reduction measures having the most significant benefit: cost ratios were determined.

Woodward-Lundgren & Associates of Oakland was selected as the consultant for Phase I, and F. Beach Leighton and Associates, Inc., provided consulting services for Phase II. No private consultant was required for Phase III.

The primary objective of the Phase I study was to develop and apply a methodology for setting priorities for geologic investigations in the urban and urbanizing areas of California. Other objectives were to establish the best means of presenting geologic information for use by planners and engineers, and to identify agencies with functions and capabilities for the solution of geologic problems in California. The objectives of Phase II were to test the methodology developed in Phase I, in five quarter quadrangles, to modify the methodology as warranted, to determine benefit:cost ratios for specific loss-reduction measures, and to prepare a draft urban geology master plan. Phase III involved the review and revision of the draft plan and, ultimately, the publication of the final project report. The methodology for setting priorities which was developed in Phase I and modified in Phase II is presented in Section 5.

Statewide Loss Projections

In order to estimate the magnitude of the total loss due to geologic hazards in California, the estimated dollar and life losses for each of the 10 geologic problems are projected for the 30-year period 1970–2000, and totaled (table 1). Total projected figures also are presented for possible amount of loss reduction, possible cost of loss-reduction measures, and benefit:cost ratios of those measures. The figures in table 1 are based on the findings of the Phase I and Phase II studies and the revisions of Phase III. The derivation of the figures is described in Section 7, Appendix A.

The 10 geologic problems are estimated to cause projected losses totaling on the order of $55 billion to the urban and urbanizing areas of California by the year 2000 if current land-use planning, development siting, building design, and construction practices are continued unchanged.

Use and Limitation of the Plan

The Urban Geology Master Plan embodied in this document, and proposed for continuing application in California, is mainly a policy plan establishing a process—framework, procedures, and policies—to guide and, hopefully, coordinate the many efforts to reduce losses from geologic hazards in California. It is designed for purposes of statewide planning. It does not establish blueprints or task-schedules for particular persons to do specific projects in a specified time schedule. The agencies of State, federal, and local governments and other organizations concerned with specific problems have been listed where deemed appropriate, partly as a guide to sources of more detailed information. The details of the various loss-reduction measures cited are not presented; too many variables are involved for such a presentation here.

This report presents some technical and administrative information designed to be directly useful to many of the agencies that deal with geologic problems in California. However, some of these data, for example the geologic hazards maps shown in figures 3 through 12, are much too generalized to be used for local planning purposes. A principal function of these small-scale maps is to indicate areas which require more detailed data and areas where the application of loss-reduction measures would be most cost effective.

The Urban Geology Master Plan attempts to speak to all persons and agencies who are concerned with the application of loss-reduction measures to geologic problems in the urban and urbanizing areas of California. This includes the Legislature and executive branch agencies in State government; executive agencies of federal government; planning, public works, engineering, and building and safety departments of local government; city councils; boards of supervisors; universities; developers; professional consultants; and the general public. This document is designed to be most informative and useful to local government agencies. The most serious gaps in the process of making geotechnical knowledge useful in reducing losses are the communications and conceptual gaps between earth science agencies and local government.

This document, therefore, seeks to improve public awareness as to: (1) what "urban geology" consists of; (2) the magnitude of geologic hazards, in terms of economics and public safety; (3) some things that should be done to reduce these hazards; and (4) how geologic information can be useful in real-life activities related to land-use planning and decisions. "Public" is intended to include citizens, industry, and responsible public agencies, both technical and administrative, both executive and legislative.

Acknowledgments

More than 200 State, federal, city and county agencies and private organizations were contacted during the course of this project; their contributions are gratefully acknowledged.

Section 3

Geologic Hazards in California

The largest losses of life
due to geologic hazards
ground shaking during earth
ing is largely due to the
during periods of sudden d
Since 1812 a total of 26 d
struck California, inflicting
and dollar property losses
dollar values at the time of t
or more than $7 billion in

Table 2. Losses due to earthq

Date	Location
1812...	San Juan Capistrano ...
1857...	Fort Tejon.........
1865...	San Francisco.........
1868...	Hayward..........
1872...	Owens Valley........
1892...	Vacaville..........
1898...	Mare Island.........
1899...	San Jacinto.........
1906...	San Francisco........
1915...	Imperial Valley
1918...	San Jacinto and Hem
1925...	Santa Barbara..
1933...	Long Beach.....
1940...	Imperial Valley.
1941...	Santa Barbara..
1941...	Torrance-Gardena
1949...	Terminal Island......
1951...	Terminal Island.......
1952...	Kern County.........
1954...	Eureka-Arcata..........
1955...	Terminal Island.......
1955...	Oakland-Walnut Creek
1957...	San Francisco.........
1961...	Terminal Island.......
1969...	Santa Rosa..........
1971...	San Fernando.........
	Totals..........

* After Coffman (1969) and the
quake Commission (1971)
** Figures reflect losses due
include other socio-economic
dollars, the total loss was
unpublished).

At present it is impossible
accurately predict earthquake
earthquakes will continue
structures must be made capable
ing forces without serious failure
and loss of life. A severe earthq
be a disaster if our structures
and built properly and if we are
effectively to the event. The
of maximum expectable earthq
fornia is shown in figure 3.

Earthquake Shaking

The largest losses of life and property in California due to geologic hazards have been caused by violent ground shaking during earthquakes. Earthquake shaking is largely due to the release of seismic energy during periods of sudden displacement along a fault. Since 1812 a total of 26 damaging earthquakes have struck California, inflicting a total life loss of 1,020 and dollar property losses in excess of $1 billion in dollar values at the time of the earthquakes (table 2), or more than $7 billion in 1971 dollar value.

*Table 2. Losses due to earthquake shaking in California.**

Date	*Location*	*Lives lost*	*Dollar loss*** *at the time of the quake*
1812	San Juan Capistrano	40	--
1857	Fort Tejon	--	--
1865	San Francisco	--	500,000
1868	Hayward	30	350,000
1872	Owens Valley	27	250,000
1892	Vacaville	--	225,000
1898	Mare Island	--	1,400,000
1899	San Jacinto	6	--
1906	San Francisco	700	500,000,000
1915	Imperial Valley	6	900,000
1918	San Jacinto and Hemet	--	200,000
1925	Santa Barbara	13	8,000,000
1933	Long Beach	115	40,000,000
1940	Imperial Valley	9	6,000,000
1941	Santa Barbara	--	100,000
1941	Torrance-Gardena	--	1,100,000
1949	Terminal Island	--	9,000,000
1951	Terminal Island	--	3,000,000
1952	Kern County	14	60,000,000
1954	Eureka-Arcata	1	2,000,000
1955	Terminal Island	--	3,000,000
1955	Oakland-Walnut Creek	1	1,000,000
1957	San Francisco	--	1,000,000
1961	Terminal Island	--	4,500,000
1969	Santa Rosa	--	8,350,000
1971	San Fernando	58	504,950,000
	Totals	1,020	$1,155,825,000

* After Coffman (1969) and the Los Angeles County Earthquake Commission (1971).

** Figures reflect losses due to property damage and do not include other socio-economic costs. If converted to 1971 dollars, the total loss would be $7,200,000,000 (Mukerjee, unpublished).

At present it is impossible to prevent, control, or accurately predict earthquakes. Therefore, since severe earthquakes will continue to occur in California, our structures must be made capable of withstanding shaking forces without serious failure and resultant injuries and loss of life. A severe earthquake does not have to be a disaster if our structures and cities are designed and built properly and if we are prepared to respond effectively to the event. The generalized distribution of maximum expectable earthquake intensity in California is shown in figure 3.

The serious concern for earthquake shaking is reflected in California by a broad range of laws and codes that have been adopted at State and local levels. The Uniform Building Code, 1970 edition, contains a seismic zone map for the United States which categorizes the country into four zones:

Zone 0—No damage

Zone 1—Minor damage. Corresponds to intensities V and VI of the Modified Mercalli scale (see table 3).

Zone 2—Moderate damage. Corresponds to VII on the Modified Mercalli scale.

Zone 3—Major damage. Corresponds to VIII or higher on the Modified Mercalli scale.

California lies entirely within Zones 2 and 3.

The map is based on the known distribution of damaging earthquakes and the Modified Mercalli intensities associated with these earthquakes; on evidence of strain release; and on considerations of major geologic structures and provinces believed to be associated with earthquake activity. The Uniform Building Code, 1970 edition, in Section 2314 describes strength and lateral force requirements for buildings in those various zones.

Photo 1. Highway overpasses that collapsed during the San Fernando earthquake of February 9, 1971. Photo courtesy Newhall Signal.

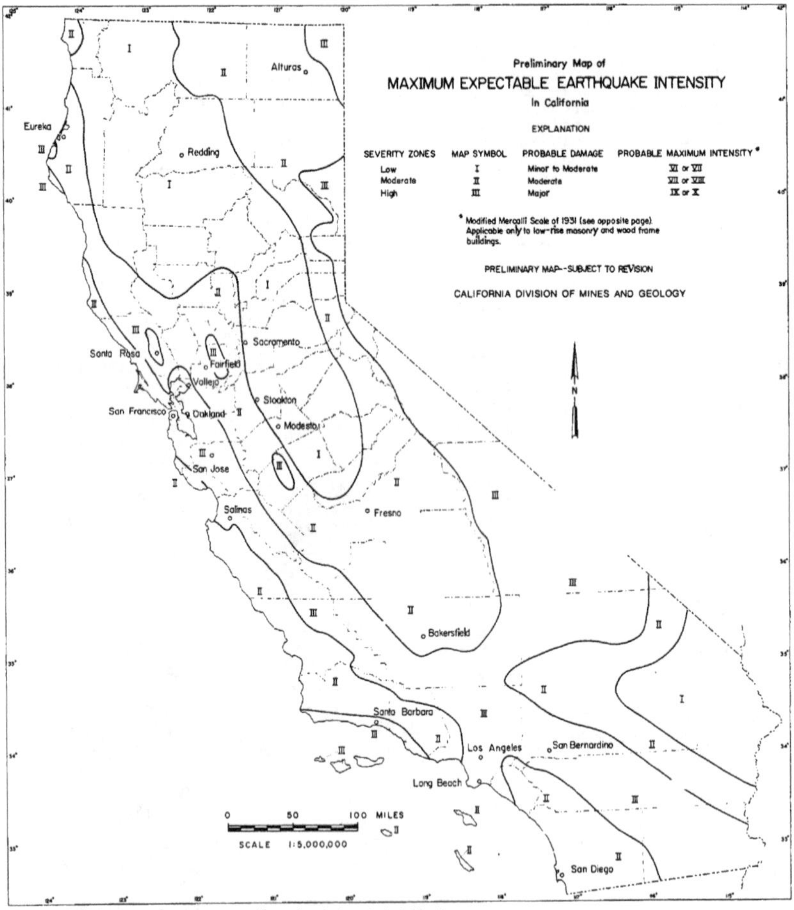

Figure 3. Preliminary map of maximum expectable earthquake intensity in California.

Table 3. Modified Mercalli scale of earthquake intensities.

THE MERCALLI INTENSITY SCALE
(As modified by Charles F. Richter in 1956 and rearranged)

If most of these effects are observed	*then the intensity is:*
Earthquake shaking not felt. But people may observe marginal effects of large distance earthquakes without identifying these effects as earthquake-caused. Among them: trees, structures, liquids, bodies of water sway slowly, or doors swing slowly.	*I*
Effect on people: Shaking felt by those at rest, especially if they are indoors, and by those on upper floors.	*II*
Effect on people: Felt by most people indoors. Some can estimate duration of shaking. But many may not recognize shaking of building as caused by an earthquake; the shaking is like that caused by the passing of light trucks.	*III*
Other effects: Hanging objects swing. *Structural effects:* Windows or doors rattle. Wooden walls and frames creak.	*IV*
Effect on people: Felt by everyone indoors. Many estimate duration of shaking. But they still may not recognize it as caused by an earthquake. The shaking is like that caused by the passing of heavy trucks, though sometimes, instead, people may feel the sensation of a jolt, as if a heavy ball had struck the walls. *Other effects:* Hanging objects swing. Standing autos rock. Crockery clashes, dishes rattle or glasses clink. *Structural effects:* Doors close, open or swing. Windows rattle.	*V*
Effect on people: Felt by everyone indoors and by most people outdoors. Many now estimate not only the duration of shaking but also its direction and have no doubt as to its cause. Sleepers wakened. *Other effects:* Hanging objects swing. Shutters or pictures move. Pendulum clocks stop, start or change rate. Standing autos rock. Crockery clashes, dishes rattle or glasses clink. Liquids disturbed, some spilled. Small unstable objects displaced or upset. *Structural effects:* Weak plaster and Masonry D* crack. Windows break. Doors close, open or swing.	*VI*
Effect on people: Felt by everyone. Many are frightened and run outdoors. People walk unsteadily. *Other effects:* Small church or school bells ring. Pictures thrown off walls, knicknacks and books off shelves. Dishes or glasses broken. Furniture moved or overturned. Trees, bushes shaken visibly, or heard to rustle. *Structural effects:* Masonry D* damaged; some cracks in Masonry C*. Weak chimneys break at roof line. Plaster, loose bricks, stones, tiles, cornices, unbraced parapets and architectural ornaments fall. Concrete irrigation ditches damaged.	*VII*
Effect on people: Difficult to stand. Shaking noticed by auto drivers. *Other effects:* Waves on ponds; water turbid with mud. Small slides and caving in along sand or gravel banks. Large bells ring. Furniture broken. Hanging objects quiver. *Structural effects:* Masonry D* heavily damaged; Masonry C* damaged, partially collapses in some cases; some damage to Masonry B*; none to Masonry A*. Stucco and some masonry walls fall. Chimneys, factory stacks, monuments, towers, elevated tanks twist or fall. Frame houses moved on foundations if not bolted down; loose panel walls thrown out. Decayed piling broken off.	*VIII*
Effect on people: General fright. People thrown to ground. *Other effects:* Changes in flow or temperature of springs and wells. Cracks in wet ground and on steep slopes. Steering of autos affected. Branches broken from trees. *Structural effects:* Masonry D* destroyed; Masonry C* heavily damaged, sometimes with complete collapse; Masonry B* is seriously damaged. General damage to foundations. Frame structures, if not bolted, shifted off foundations. Frames racked. Reservoirs seriously damaged. Underground pipes broken.	*IX*
Effect on people: General Panic. *Other effects:* Conspicuous cracks in ground. In areas of soft ground, sand is ejected through holes and piles up into a small crater, and, in muddy areas, water fountains are formed. *Structural effects:* Most masonry and frame structures destroyed along with their foundations. Some well-built wooden structures and bridges destroyed. Serious damage to dams, dikes and embankments. Railroads bent slightly.	*X*
Effect on people: General panic. *Other effects:* Large landslides. Water thrown on banks of canals, rivers, lakes, etc. Sand and mud shifted horizontally on beaches and flat land. *Structural effects:* General destruction of buildings. Underground pipelines completely out of service. Railroads bent greatly.	*XI*
Effect on people: General panic. *Other effects:* Same as for Intensity X. *Structural effects:* Damage nearly total, the ultimate catastrophe. *Other effects:* Large rock masses displaced. Lines of sight and level distorted. Objects thrown into air.	*XII*

* Masonry A: Good workmanship and mortar, reinforced, designed to resist lateral forces.
Masonry B: Good workmanship and mortar, reinforced.
Masonry C: Good workmanship and mortar, unreinforced.
Masonry D: Poor workmanship and mortar and weak materials, like adobe.

Photo 2. Aerial view of the damage at the Sylmar Veterans Administration Hospital caused by the February 9, 1971, San Fernando earthquake. *Los Angeles Times* photo.

In recent years, many cities have enacted ordinances to deal with specific local problems. Parapet ordinances, aimed at strengthening or removing projections and appendages on the tops and along the sides of buildings, have been passed by the cities of Los Angeles and San Francisco. However, in San Francisco, funds have not been made available to allow implementation and enforcement of the ordinance. The City of Long Beach has extended its Municipal Code to include the inspection and evaluation of all buildings used for human occupancy. Buildings having inadequate resistance to lateral forces must be strengthened, demolished, or converted to a use involving a lower human-occupancy factor (Long Beach Municipal Code Section 8100).

State regulation with regard to building and earthquake shaking was begun following the 1933 Long Beach earthquake. The Field and Riley Acts were passed that year and the State Office of Architecture and Construction was established under the Department of General Services. The Field Act (Education Code Section 15451–15466) placed the design of schools under the direct supervision of the Office of Architecture and Construction .The Riley Act (Health and Safety Code Section 19100–19170) placed design requirements on other buildings used for human occupancy except dwellings designed for two families or less. The requirements of this act are enforced by county building officials.

More recently, planning laws have been used as a method for reducing earthquake damage. In 1971, the State enacted legislation requiring cities and counties to include a seismic safety element in their general plans (Government Code Section 65302). This element consists of "an identification and appraisal of seismic hazards such as susceptibility to surface ruptures from faulting, to ground shaking, to ground failures, or to effects of seismically induced waves such as tsunamis and seiches."

Recommendations for reducing losses in future earthquakes have been developed by the Governor's Earthquake Council (1972); other recommendations are under development by the Joint Committee on Seismic Safety of the California Legislature.

An enlightening report has recently been completed on the probable results of a major earthquake in the San Francisco Bay area (Algermissen *et al.*, 1972). This study postulates earthquakes to magnitude 8.3

on the San Andreas and Hayward faults, with epicenters near the San Francisco and East Bay metropolitan areas, and at different times of day. It considers the probable effects and demands on medical resources including hospitals, supplies, laboratories, and ambulance services, as well as probable effects on public needs such as communications, transportation, utilities, schools, and mercantile areas. Deaths and injuries are estimated for various earthquake magnitudes at different times of the day as follows (Algermissen, *et al.*, 1972, table 50, p. 121).

	Magnitude	Time	Deaths*	Hospitalized injuries
San Andreas fault..	8.3	2:30 a.m.	2,850	10,800
		2:00 p.m.	9,640	34,400
		4:30 p.m.	10,360	40,360
	7	2:30 a.m.	500	1,900
		2:00 p.m.	1,640	6,200
		4:30 p.m.	1,990	11,680
	6	2:30 a.m.	25	100
		2:00 p.m.	80	320
		4:30 p.m.	100	390
Hayward fault.....	8.3	2:30 a.m.	3,120	11,600
		2:00 p.m.	7,200	28,500
		4:30 p.m.	6,650	24,900
	7	2:30 a.m.	1,040	3,860
		2:00 p.m.	3,200	9,900
		4:30 p.m.	2,240	8,160
	6	2:30 a.m.	330	1,220
		2:00 p.m.	730	2,600
		4:30 p.m.	700	2,550

* Deaths in the event of dam failure are not included.

In addition to life loss and injuries, major social disruptions are probable for the largest earthquake although not for the lesser ones.

Loss of Mineral Resources

The loss of mineral deposits to urbanization is not a geologic "hazard" in that life loss and property damages are not involved, but it constitutes a significant portion of the total loss attributable to geologic problems. As urban expansion continues in California, useful minerals of all kinds are being covered by residential, commercial and public development and as such are removed from our inventory of available materials. In other cases, access to and from mineral deposits becomes difficult or impossible, with the same effect. Some minerals can be mined elsewhere, but usually at a greater cost. Other minerals, however, may not be found elsewhere or if they are found, may not be of sufficient quantity and quality to warrant exploitation. Figure 4 shows the generalized distribution of known significant mineral deposits in California.

In order to be conserved, significant mineral deposits must be recognized and protected prior to and during mining. Recognition and assessment of mineral deposits is the job of mining geologists who may be employed by private mining companies, the California Division of Mines and Geology, the U.S. Geological Survey, the U.S. Bureau of Mines, or the U.S. Bureau of Land Management. Protection of important deposits becomes the responsibility of city and county government.

Once a mineral inventory has been completed, significant mineral deposits can be compared in value to the alternative land use options threatening them. Many variations of land use management may be followed in such instances by local government. These variations might include:

1. The extraction of a mineral deposit and the subsequent use of the reclaimed land for some other purpose. For example, hillside quarries can be graded into building sites and open pits can be converted to recreational lakes, waste disposal sites, and other beneficial uses.
2. Subsurface mineral extraction with the surface committed to other land use. For example, petroleum has been produced from beneath the City of Los Angeles for many years without adverse effects, except for some subsidence, now alleviated, along limited sections of the coastline. Underground mining has been conducted under many of

Photo 3. Worked-out gravel pits in the Livermore Valley. Some of these pits have been converted to recreation lakes after being depleted. *Kaiser Industries photo.*

the towns of the Mother Lode without adverse surface effects.

3. **The protection of special mineral deposits. Some mineral deposits should be placed in protective mining use zones and reserved for this purpose. An example is the New Almaden mercury mine near San Jose. This mine has been the largest single producer of mercury in the United States (more than one-third of the national total) and considerable low-grade ore remains. Although the deposit cannot be worked at present metal prices, ore resources should be reserved for future use.**

4. **The setting aside of some mineral materials areas where mineral products are so low in unit cost yet so expensive to transport that they must be produced in areas located close to points of end use. Sand and gravel for concrete aggregate is a good example of this. As existing deposits are worked out or threatened by competing land uses, new deposits must be located at distances farther from places of use. Each such move increases the cost of the product about four cents per ton for each mile of truck transport. At 25 to 30 miles, the cost of transportation by truck, the most common means, may equal or exceed the value of the sand and gravel. For these reasons, it would be desirable to protect specific deposits for mining use and maintain access routes until deposits are depleted and the land can be reclaimed for alternative uses.**

It is the continuing policy of the State of California to foster and encourage the orderly development and utilization of the state's mineral resources (Section 2650, Public Resources Code). Section 65302 of the Government Code requires that the general plan of each city and county contain a conservation element for the conservation, development, and utilization of natural resources including minerals. Some counties and cities have established mineral or natural resource zones to protect and provide for the orderly development of mineral deposits.

No figures have been tabulated relating to the cost of mineral deposits lost to urbanization to date but, if known, amounts would certainly be substantial. The value of many mineral materials is sufficiently high that proportional costs of additional transportation are low or even negligible. These conditions do not apply, however, to low-cost materials used in construction. At points of production, sand, gravel, and crushed stone range in price from $1.25 to $2.00 per ton and haulage is a critical cost factor in production economics. With continued loss of mineral properties to urbanization, it is estimated that most present producers will have to move their operations to new

Photo 4. An artificial island near Long Beach used for petroleum production. *Photo by City of Long Beach, Department of Oil Properties.*

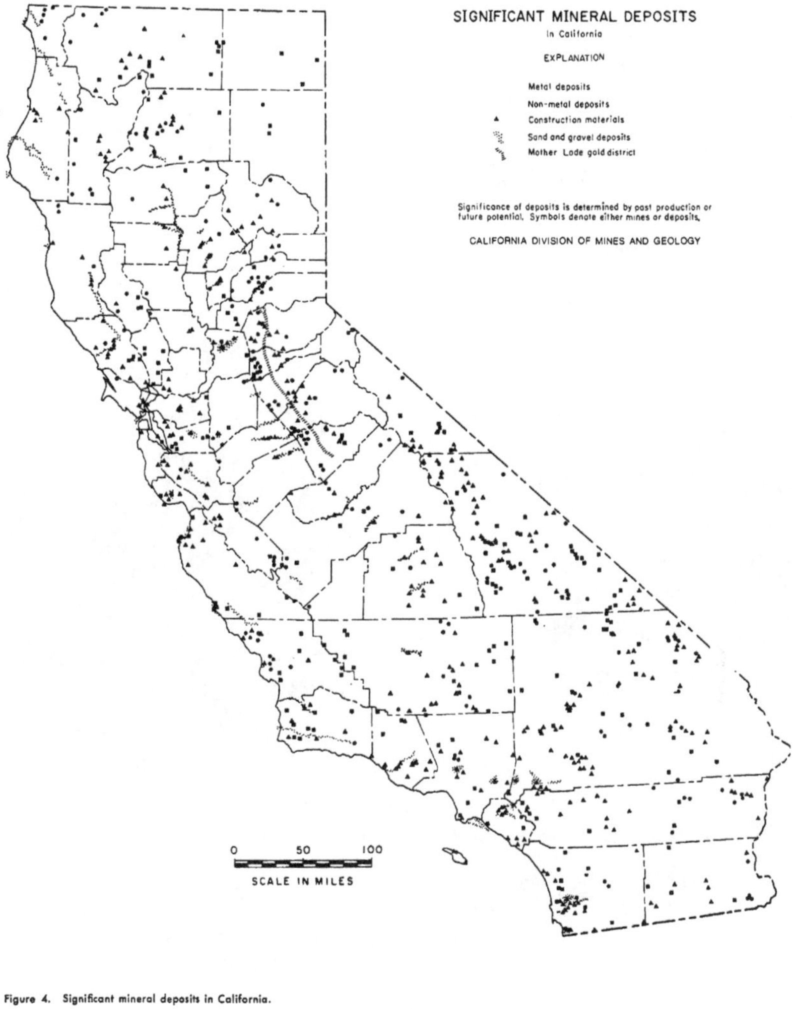

Figure 4. Significant mineral deposits in California.

deposits averaging 25 miles farther from points of consumer use by the year 2000 and that the transportation costs are estimated to increase to about nine cents per ton mile. The additional costs for truck haulage will thus be $3.50 per ton in the year 2000.

Appraisals and inventories of important mineral deposits should be made throughout the state. Special attention should be given to construction materials so that future needs can be filled without unneeded expense. Mineral deposits needed for the continued economic development of California should be provided with appropriate zoning and access protection.

Appropriate ordinances should be adopted, to assure that 1) adjacent land is not adversely affected by the mining operation, and 2) the depleted mineral land is reclaimed after exploitation.

Landsliding

A landslide is the downhill movement of masses of earth material under the force of gravity. Movement may be rapid or so slow that a change of position can be noted only over a period of weeks or years. The areal size of a landslide can range from several square feet to several square miles. Slide thicknesses may range from less than a foot to several hundred feet. Landslides are a common problem in the hillside areas of California and, in terms of dollar losses, are one of the more costly geologic hazards. Figure 5 shows the relative amounts of landslides throughout California.

Damage due to landslides can be reduced in areas undergoing development by such alternatives as avoidance, removal, or permanent stabilization of slide masses. In all cases, a first and critical step is to recognize the existence of an old slide or the probability of a future slide. This is accomplished through detailed geologic mapping, trenching, drilling, and frequently the photo-interpretation of surface geologic conditions. Old slides can be recognized by their lobe-like forms and the track-like hollows which they leave behind them. Probable future slides can often be anticipated in areas where other landsliding has already taken place. Slopes covered with deep soils or hillsides heavily saturated with ground water are potential slide areas. Where bedding or jointing of rock materials and hill slope directions tend to be the same, slide possibilities are greatly increased. Fault zones regardless of recency of movement are also generally potential landslide areas.

Geologic mapping of landslides in California by field and photo-interpretation techniques is presently

Photo 5. Landslide along the coastal bluffs in the city of San Clemente, Orange County. Photo by George B. Cleveland.

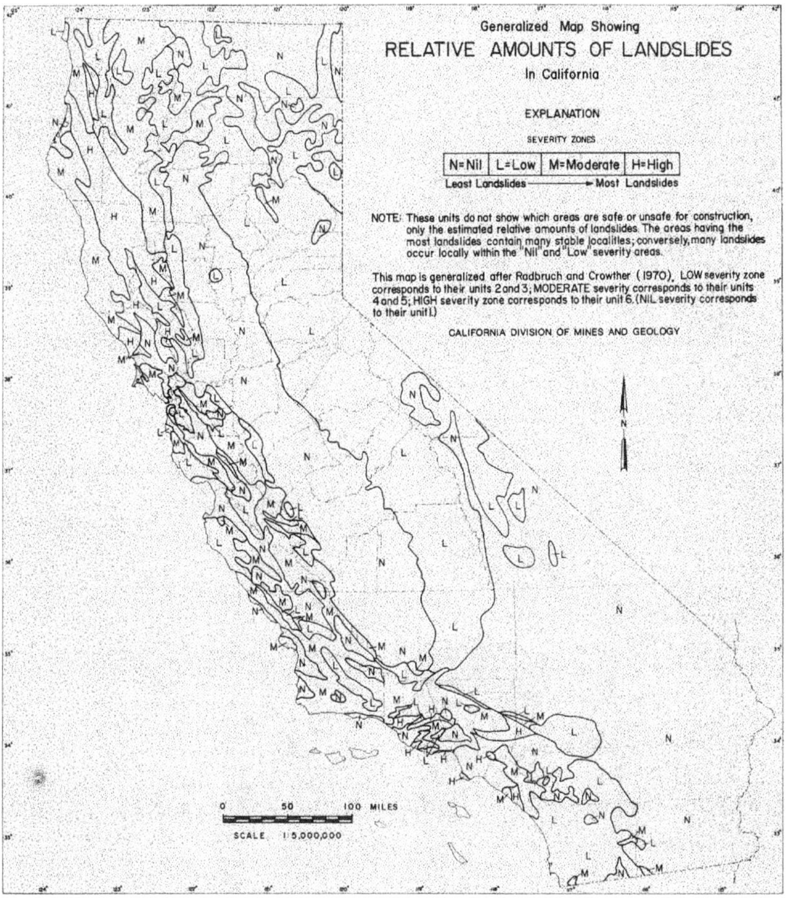

Figure 5. Generalized map showing relative amounts of landslides in California.

conducted by several groups of trained geologists including:

1. **The California Division of Mines and Geology, the U.S. Geological Survey, and other public agencies. The results of studies by these organizations are used by local government and developers to appraise the overall severity of landsliding in many areas of California.**
2. **Consulting geologists. Detailed site studies for developments are conducted by consulting geologists hired by developers. In some jurisdictions these studies are required by planning or building safety officials of local government to assure public safety and to reduce or eliminate losses to roads and other improvements maintained by local government when development is completed.**

After the landslide potential has been recognized and assessed at a site, future development is designed to take landslide hazards in the area into consideration. Much landslide damage can be avoided simply by leaving hazardous areas undeveloped. Small landslides may be totally removed and soil materials used elsewhere as compacted fill. Stabilization may be accomplished by:

1. **Dewatering the slide by installing drainage devices.**
2. **Buttressing slide toes and sides with compacted soil or retaining walls.**
3. **Removing and redistributing some or all of the landslide debris, especially from the head of the slide.**

Some early efforts at chemical stabilization also show promise.

Existing State legislation treats landslides, along with earthquakes, under the general category of geologic hazards. Section 15002.1 of the Education Code requires the governing board of a school district to have proposed school sites studied in order to detect the presence of unfavorable geological characteristics. Section 65302.1 of the Government Code requires that each general plan include a safety element. This element requires, among other things, protection of the community from geologic hazards and geologic hazard mapping in areas of known geologic hazards.

Inspection and control of siting and development activities so as to prevent subsequent landslide damage should be and, in some areas, are carried out at the local government level through the adoption of some form of a grading ordinance. A common method is to adopt Chapter 70 of the Uniform Building Code, or more stringent grading ordinances adapted to local needs and circumstances.

Photo 6. Homes destroyed by landsliding of artificial fill on the north slope of Palos Verdes Hills, Los Angeles County. Photo by *George B. Cleveland.*

EXAMPLES OF LOSSES

The Portugese Bend landslide is located on the Palos Verdes peninsula in southwestern Los Angeles County. An old slide was reactivated in 1956 on a 170-acre swath of land extending from near the western summit of the Palos Verdes Hills down to the Pacific Ocean. This slide has damaged or destroyed more than 200 homes. In February 1973, in the area of maximum movement, it was moving at an average rate of one foot per month.

The affected homeowners banded together and filed suits (Los Angeles Superior Court Case No. 684595 and consolidated cases) against the Los Angeles County Road Department, charging that the slide had been activated by an extension of Crenshaw Boulevard. The Court found that the County was liable and established two points:

1. **That road construction carried out by the County may have initiated movement on the slide.**
2. **That the County was better able to support the loss than were the individual home owners.**

The losses amounted to approximately $6,000,000 and, with accumulated interest, the final settlement was close to $7,000,000.

When the County was charged with this suit, it found itself in the difficult position of having no in-house staff to offer technical advice as to what had happened. In order to fill this void, an engineering geology section was established within the Design Division of the Office of the County Engineer. This section, operating on an average budget of $75,000 per year, now carries out geologic and engineering functions regarding building foundation conditions and advises on the geologic safety of road construction throughout Los Angeles County.

Because of the relatively weak rocks and steep slopes found in many areas, the City of Los Angeles has had a long history of damage due to landslides. When developed, these areas in the past have experienced many slides, especially during periods of heavy and prolonged rainfall. The city met this problem by using grading ordinances which have, from their inception in 1952 to the present time, become progressively more comprehensive: Major tests of these grading ordinances occurred during the heavy rain years of 1952, 1957, 1962 and 1969. Major changes in the grading code were instituted in the following periods:

1. **Pre-1952—No grading code was in effect, therefore little or no soils engineering and no engineering geology was done.**
2. **1952–1962—A moderately effective grading ordinance was in effect requiring soils engineering but very limited geologic evaluation.**
3. **1963 to present—A modern grading ordinance was in effect requiring soils engineering and engineering geology through all design and construction stages.**

Data on these different stages were collected by Charles A. Yelverton, formerly of the Los Angeles Department of Building and Safety, based on the storm year of 1969; and James E. Slosson prepared cost and effectiveness figures.

During the early stage, when no grading ordinance was in effect, approximately 10,000 hillside lots were developed. Of these, 1,040 failed in 1969 for a total loss of $3,300,000 during this single storm year. The average damage was $330 per developed hillside lot and failures occurred on 10.4 percent of the lots. In the 1952–1962 period, 27,000 sites were developed. Of these, 350 were damaged in 1969 for a total loss of $2,767,000. The average damage was slightly over $100 per developed lot and the failure rate had dropped to 1.3 percent. After 1963, 11,000 sites were developed; 17 (some of which were under construction) were damaged in 1969 for a loss of $182,400. The average loss per developed site was $7 and the loss rate was 0.15 percent.

These figures indicate that the loss rate can be reduced from 10.4 percent to 0.15 percent through the use of an effective grading ordinance. The percentage improvement is 98.6 percent. This improvement involves some additional costs, however. The developer incurs additional design costs averaging $243 per lot; additional grading costs average $500 per lot; and city inspection costs average $335 per lot for a total additional cost of $1,078 per lot or about 10 percent of the average losses without control. This is substantially less than the 10.4 percent pre-1952 loss rate.

The U.S. Geological Survey has compiled loss figures (Taylor and Brabb, 1972) for landslide losses in the S.F. Bay Area counties for the 1968–1969 storm year. The total losses, which they consider to be low by an unknown factor, were $25,393,956. In general, the Bay Area counties do not have geological staffs to review geologic reports or to inspect geologic conditions at developments.

Experience has shown that landslide losses can be reduced to about 1 percent by early recognition of potential problems and careful, controlled design. The steps needed to bring about significant reductions in losses are:

1. The delineation of landslides and landslide-prone areas on a geologic map of the area on a scale of 1:24,000 or larger. Special attention should be given to surficial units and slope stability factors including weak rock types, slope angle, drainage, rainfall and vegetation type.
2. The guiding of development, through the planning process, into those areas having the fewest economically uncorrectable problems.
3. The requiring of the land developer to use engineering geology practices and soils engineering methods throughout his design. Existing or potential landslides should be corrected or avoided.
4. The establishment of a grading division within the local government structure to enforce the grading ordinance (Chapter 70, Uniform Building Code) and to represent the city and county interests in safe development. This group should review and approve development plans from preliminary to the final stages and should inspect the grading to insure that design requirements are actually carried out.

Flooding

Flooding is one of the costliest natural hazards in California. National statistics show that California ranks as one of the major flood problem areas in the nation and that flooding is one of the principal factors to be considered in the overall development and use of land resources. Although existing flood control measures have, in general, been effective in controlling or reducing flood damages, flood problems have nonetheless continued to grow. The distribution of areas subject to flooding in California is shown in figure 6.

The earliest recorded California flood was reported by Father Juan Crespi when a flood on the Los Angeles River caused the river to change its course in 1770. Between 1770 and 1950, 23 major floods have been recorded at various locations in the state, claiming 144 lives in the 50 years from 1900 to 1950. The greatest of these were:

1805 —The inundation of the entire floor of the Great Valley, causing great loss of life and destruction of Indian villages.

1861–62—The inundation of the Great Valley, the Los Angeles basin, and other areas in the state.

1907 —The flooding of northern California and the Great Valley.

1909 —The flooding of northern California and over 300,000 acres in the Great Valley.

Since 1950 there have been 11 major floods with the loss of 222 lives and extensive damage to property (California Region Framework Study Committee, 1971).

Flooding events are of two main types:

1. Off-site flooding, caused by rain or snow-melt water from up-stream watersheds.
2. On-site flooding caused by the runoff of water in local areas.

Off-site flooding may involve large volumes of water and is a frequent cause of flood damage in California. Federal, State and regional agencies have developed large and sophisticated programs to cope with this type of flooding on a long-term basis. On-site flooding is basically the responsibility of county and city governments, commonly acting through local flood control districts.

The numerous programs for reducing flood losses include both structural and nonstructural approaches, some directed at preventing floods, others at controlling those that cannot be prevented. Structural measures include flood-water storage systems such as dams, reservoirs, basins, and the construction of related facilities such as levees and channel developments. Watershed land treatment may also be carried out to reduce runoff, debris movement, erosion, and sedimentation. Nonstructural measures include flood forecasting, zoning and subdivision regulations, the exclusion of use in primary floodways, building code requirements, and the evacuation of flood areas. For many agricultural and developed urban centers, structural measures are most feasible; for emerging communities, however, non-structural measures appear to be more effective.

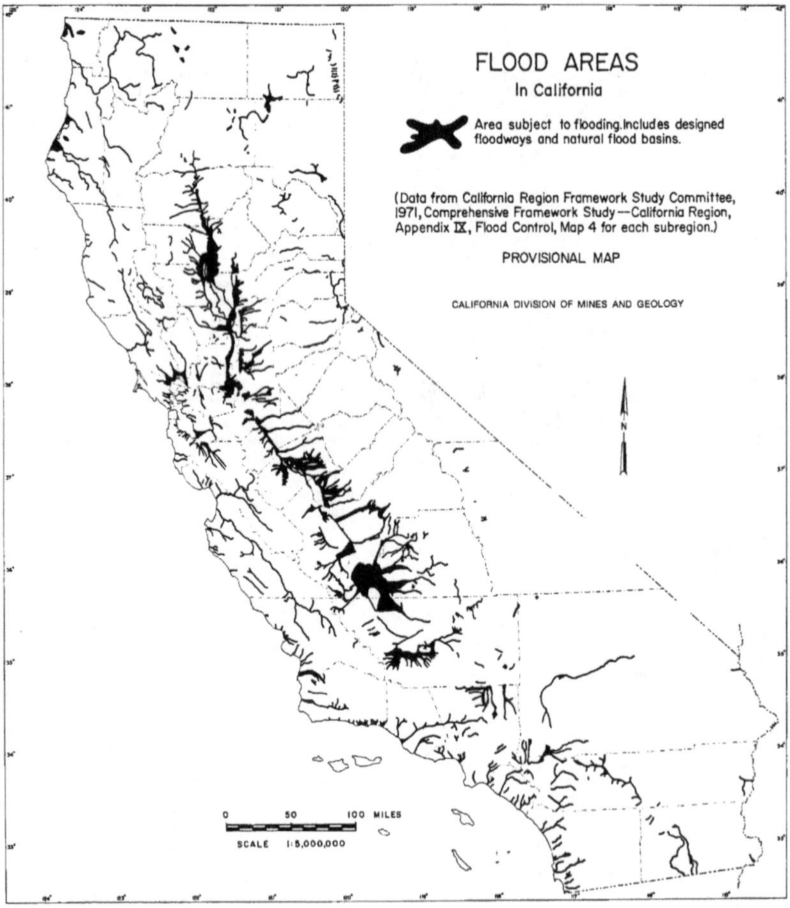
FLOOD AREAS
In California
Area subject to flooding. Includes designed floodways and natural flood basins.
(Data from California Region Framework Study Committee, 1971, Comprehensive Framework Study—California Region, Appendix IX, Flood Control, Map 4 for each subregion.)
PROVISIONAL MAP
CALIFORNIA DIVISION OF MINES AND GEOLOGY
N
0 50 100 MILES
SCALE 1:5,000,000

Figure 6. Flood areas in California.

The California Region Framework Study Committee (1971) has sketched out a multi-faceted program for controlling flood damage in California until the year 2020. This program is calculated to hold the level of unprevented flood damage approximately constant ($100–120 million per year), while program costs would decrease $100–64 million per year). Over the 50-year period, in which California's population is expected to increase threefold, damages without the proposed measures would otherwise increase sixfold. This program mainly foresees the continuation of established measures under present agency responsibilities. Structural control measures would be the prime responsibility of the U.S. Army Corps of Engineers and the California Department of Water Resources. Flood forecasting would be conducted by the National Weather Service and the Department of Water Resources.

There are other specific non-structural needs which would further reduce flooding losses. Improvements in weather science could allow quantitative, short-term precipitation forecasts in a particular watershed. The art of flood forecasting, based mainly on hydrology, is ahead of weather forecasting in the sense that flood crest times can be accurately predicted if precipitation distributions are known.

There is a need for effective zoning procedures under which controls could be exercised over the uses permitted in designated floodways. Zoning is primarily a political problem, and the authority to establish and enforce zoning laws effectively lies with local government. Potential flood boundaries can be established, through techniques of hydrology, but authorities in local government must exercise control in the land use planning of hazardous areas. Local government should prohibit, by ordinance and/or zoning, urban or commercial development in a flood-prone zone unless flood control facilities are provided.

Flooding has long been recognized as a serious problem in California and many laws relating to flooding are now in effect within the state. The Subdivision Map Act specifies that the Division of Real Estate may refuse approval of a subdivision if it is threatened by flooding (Sec. 11551.5, Business and Professions

Photo 7. The Sacramento River flooding Sherman Island, 1969. *California Department of Water Resources photo.*

Code). Prospective school sites must have suitable engineering work done to assure that surface drainage conditions have been considered (Sec. 15002.1, Education Code). Flooding must be considered in several elements of the general plan and these include:

Land use element—requires the identification of areas subject to flooding.

Conservation element—suggests considering the conservation aspects of flood control.

Erosion Activity

Erosion generally involves two somewhat distinct problems—the wear and removal of material from one site and its deposition at another. The removal of soils through erosion can be damaging in situations of sheet and gully erosion of land surfaces; the wind-blown denudation of lands; the erosion of stream courses and banks; and the erosion of coastal cliffs, dunes and beach areas. Deposition damage affects flood plains, rivers, lakes, reservoirs, and may clog drainage structures. Activities by man frequently accelerate erosion-related damages and losses.

Erosion-prevention measures and their costs are commonly included in the grading and land-engineering practices designed to prevent landsliding and expansive soil problems. Sediment removal costs rarely show whether a problem was caused by "erosion," "landsliding," or "flooding." Broad classifications have obscured the real costs of erosion damage and have also obscured the actual costs of prevention and control. The rendering of benefit:cost analyses of erosion problems, therefore, is made virtually impossible.

Erosion is a relatively well understood and controllable problem insofar as it affects urban areas. The vulnerability of natural soil types to erosion (erodibility) has been mapped by the U.S. Soil Conservation Service and other soils surveys, especially in more recent projects completed since 1960. The generalized distribution of erosion activity in California is shown in figure 7. In most areas undergoing development, however, the natural erodibility of the soil is far less important in determining the severity of future erosion than is the type and amount of land-modification being performed.

The reduction of erosion losses in urban areas is the responsibility of both the developer who modifies the land surface by landscaping and construction of retaining walls and drainage systems and the governmental agency which reviews and, to some extent, controls land modification. Following project completion, the user of the property assumes the continuing responsibility of erosion control through maintenance of landscaping and drainage systems.

Erosion problems in urban areas of California are, for the most part, well under control in those areas where appropriate engineering practices are properly applied. In localities where erosion cannot feasibly be prevented or controlled, moderate losses will continue to occur. Most urban areas however, have public works capabilities fully able to cope with erosion problems.

The preventive costs of erosion are generally included within flood control measures and in the overall costs of hillside development. Adoption of the present state-of-the-art procedures for landslide prevention in hillside areas will, in most cases, eliminate losses brought about through erosion.

Photo 8. Erosion associated with road construction. ***U.S. Soil Conservation Service photo.***

Expansive Soils

Expansive soils are earth materials which greatly increase in volume when they absorb water and shrink when they dry out. Expansion is most often caused by clay minerals, primarily montmorillonite and illite. Although not common, expansive rocks are also known; these are claystones or altered volcanic tuffs which contain large proportions of montmorillonite. The basic cause of expansion is the attraction and absorption of water into the expansible crystal lattices of the clay minerals. The water may be derived from moisture in the air or ground water beneath the foundations of buildings. When buildings are placed on expansive soils, foundations may rise each wet season and fall each dry season. Movements may vary under different parts of a building with the result that foundations crack, various structural portions of the building are distorted, and doors and windows are warped so that they do not function properly. The generalized distribution of expansive soils in California is shown in figure 8.

The adverse effects of expansive soils can be avoided through proper drainage and foundation design. In order to design an adequate foundation, however, the condition must be recognized through appropriate laboratory soils testing. Expansive soils are recognized through expansion tests of samples of soil or rock, or by means of the interpretation of Atterberg limits tests, a standard soils testing procedure.

Expansive soils are studied on a regional basis by soils scientists of the U.S. Soil Conservation Service and the U.S. Forest Service. Building site evaluations are normally conducted by consulting soils or foundation engineers retained by developers.

Procedures employed in expansive soils testing are found in many codes and regulations. Chapter 70 of the Uniform Building Code requires that soils testing

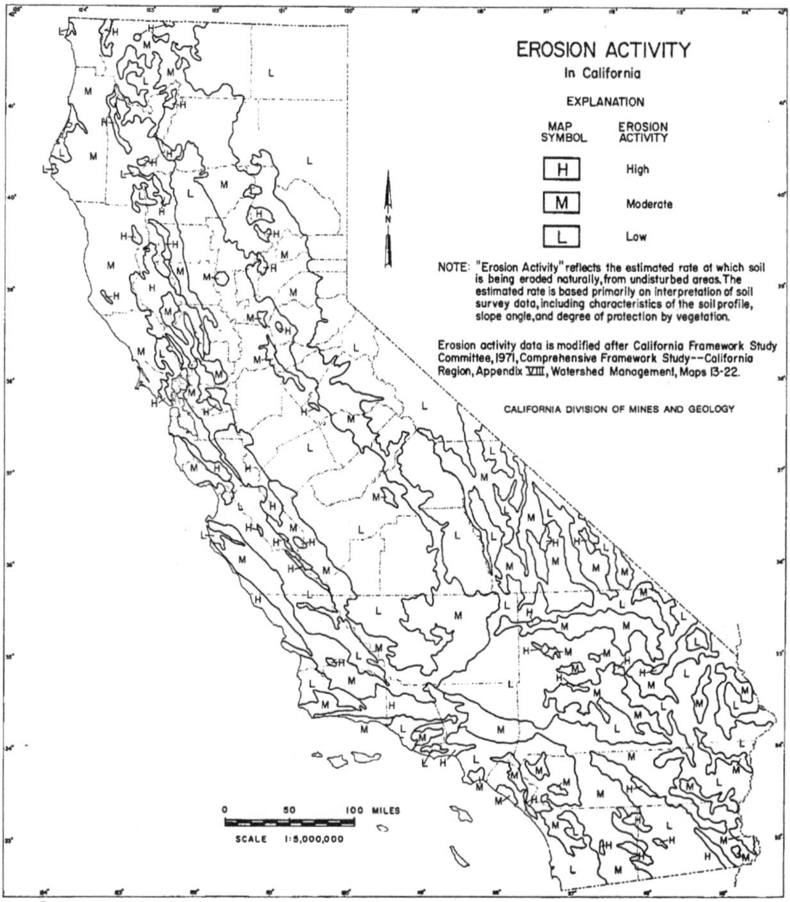
EROSION ACTIVITY
In California
EXPLANATION
MAP SYMBOL
EROSION ACTIVITY
H High
M Moderate
L Low
NOTE: "Erosion Activity" reflects the estimated rate at which soil is being eroded naturally, from undisturbed areas. The estimated rate is based primarily on interpretation of soil survey data, including characteristics of the soil profile, slope angle, and degree of protection by vegetation.
Erosion activity data is modified after California Framework Study Committee, 1971, Comprehensive Framework Study--California Region, Appendix VIII, Watershed Management, Maps 13-22.
CALIFORNIA DIVISION OF MINES AND GEOLOGY
0 50 100 MILES
SCALE 1:5,000,000

Figure 7. Erosion activity in California.

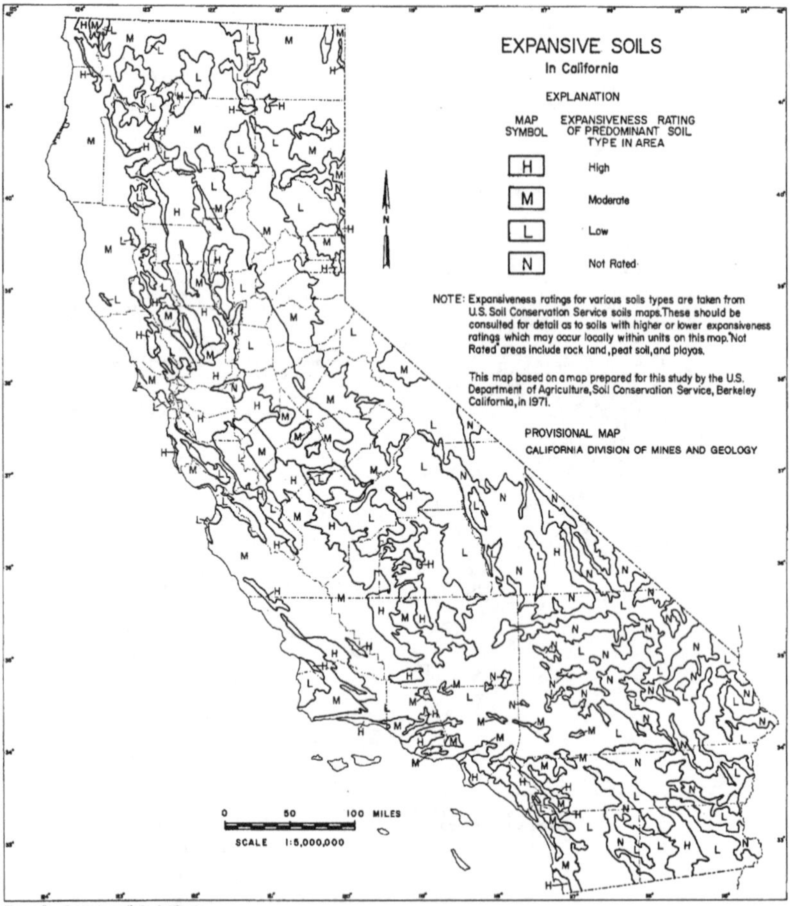
EXPANSIVE SOILS
In California
EXPLANATION
MAP SYMBOL
EXPANSIVENESS RATING OF PREDOMINANT SOIL TYPE IN AREA
H High
M Moderate
L Low
N Not Rated
NOTE: Expansiveness ratings for various soils types are taken from U.S. Soil Conservation Service soils maps. These should be consulted for detail as to soils with higher or lower expansiveness ratings which may occur locally within units on this map. "Not Rated" areas include rock land, peat soil, and playas.
This map based on a map prepared for this study by the U.S. Department of Agriculture, Soil Conservation Service, Berkeley California, in 1971.
PROVISIONAL MAP
CALIFORNIA DIVISION OF MINES AND GEOLOGY
0 50 100 MILES
SCALE 1:5,000,000

Figure 8. Expansive soils in California.

Photo 9. Erosion control measures used in a southern California subdivision. Narrow terraces and pipes are being used to bring water from the building sites safely down the hill. *County of Los Angeles photo.*

be done on all graded building sites. Soils tests are also required by other local building codes and by lending institutions (including the Veterans Administration and the Federal Housing Administration) on new building sites. The Subdivision Map Act of the Business and Professions Code (Section 11010) requires that on all tract developments of five lots or more, soil conditions be studied by a registered civil engineer unless waived by the local government building official. By following a variety of test procedures, a qualified engineer can detect the presence of expansive soils and recommend needed corrective measures.

Once expansive soils have been recognized as a potential problem, corrective measures can be designed into the foundation for little additional cost. Depending upon the soils situation, examples of corrective measures are as follows: *

1. Compaction and water content of the building site can be designed to allow for some open spaces or voids. The voids will permit some expansion to take place within the soil mass and will prevent expansion of the entire graded section. Compaction to 85 percent of maximum optimum density with water contents several percent above optimum will commonly accomplish this.
2. The moisture content can be stabilized by soaking the building site and maintaining this water content during and after construction.
3. Concrete slab floors can be strengthened by increasing their thickness and including reinforcing steel. This will allow the foundation to rise and fall as a unit.
4. Drains and water barriers can be installed around and under foundations to prevent water from entering the foundation area.
5. The building foundations can be extended downward by piers so that building structures rest on underlying non-expansive materials. The piers can be tied together by grade beams that unite the foundation into a more rigid unit.
6. Gravel blankets have been used under concrete slabs.

The costs involved in recognizing and correcting expansive soils usually are not great. Using a 35-to-50 home subdivision as a basis for evaluation, soil testing will average $6 to $10 per lot; grading $15 to $25 per lot; and soaking $4 to $5 per lot. Strengthening a slab floor costs approximately 30¢ per square foot or $450 for an average structure of 1500 square feet. Pier and grade beams may not necessarily cost more than a standard foundation, although they may cost several hundred dollars more than a minimum acceptable foundation.

Foundations in expansive rock can be comparatively expensive, because deep piers must be used to place building weights below zones of expansive rock materials. In some instances, "water blocking" may be required. Additional foundation costs of $2,000 to $8,000 can be involved, and engineering costs can run as high as $2,000.

Corrective costs after construction can be high compared to preventive costs carried out before construction. In some problem areas, chemical stabilization (such as lime injection) can be effective. More often a new foundation must be placed beneath the existing structure and costs can amount to 25 percent of the total value of the building. Nonetheless, new foundations may be justified because damage due to expansive soils can reduce the value of a building by 10 to 80 percent.

* Information supplied by Gery Anderson, Geomechanics Inc., Sacramento.

Photo 10. Urban development along the San Andreas fault zone south of San Francisco. The fault zone extends from sag pond in lower left of photo to upper center. *Photo by Marshall Moxom.*

At the present time, adequate techniques are in existence to control damage from expansive soils and expansive bedrock, but regulatory vigilance should be maintained and improved to assure that site investigations and, if warranted, proper engineering are carried out before construction. If existing ordinances are rigorously enforced, losses to future construction could be reduced to near-negligible levels.

Fault Displacement

A fault is a fracture in the crust of the earth along which the sides have moved or been displaced, relative to each other, in a direction parallel to the fracture. Active faults are the main sources of earthquakes. Land use planners should consider the possible future effects of fault movement in conjunction with the placement and design of new structures. Two aspects of fault displacement should be considered:

1. The effects that sudden displacement along faults may have on structures built across their traces.
2. The relatively slow effects of fault creep—the gradual ground distortion and movement along a fault trace not accompanied by significant earthquakes.

Fault displacements involve forces so great that the only means of limiting damage to man-made structures is to avoid areas along traces of active faulting or to design structures to accommodate the expected displacement. In order to avoid faults they must be recognized. All active and potentially active faults have not been located and mapped. This normally is done through geologic mapping and subsurface investigation. Although there are thousands of faults—both large and small—in California, most of these are no longer active and are not likely to be subject to further displacement. Regional studies of fault activity are conducted principally by geologists of the California Division of Mines and Geology, the U.S. Geological Survey and universities; detailed site investigations are conducted by consulting geologists. Figure 9 shows the distribution of faults in California which have have had historic and Quaternary displacement.

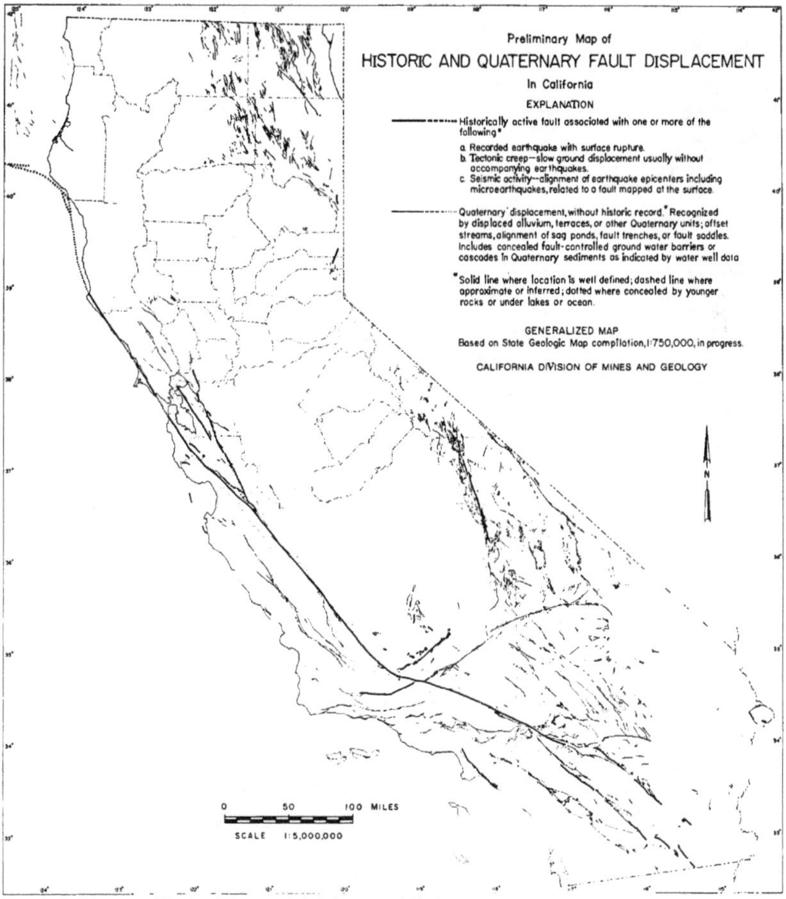

Figure 9. Preliminary map of historic and Quaternary fault displacement in California.

Photo 11. Fault displacement resulting from the San Fernando earthquake of February 9, 1971. *Photo by James E. Kahle.*

Once the trace of an active fault has been recognized, the consulting geologist must advise the developer of the relative risks to developments constructed at different distances from the fault trace. It may be that certain high-risk areas should not be developed. Unfortunately, there are few development guidelines because so little is known concerning the detailed effects of fault displacement. Swaths of no development along active fault traces, as narrow as 20 feet and as wide as 350 feet, have been recommended.

Existing State legislation treats fault displacement under the general category of geologic hazards. Section 65302 of the Government Code requires each general plan to contain a seismic safety element including, among other items, the "identification and appraisal of seismic hazards such as susceptibility to surface ruptures from faulting." Section 15002.1 of the State Education Code requires the governing board of any school district to have proposed school sites studied in order to detect the presence of unfavorable geological characteristics. Both laws require appraisals of surface ruptures from faulting, the protection of the community from geologic hazards, and geologic mapping in areas of known geologic hazards.

The recently enacted Alquist-Priolo Geologic Hazard Zones Act (Chapter 7.5, Division 2, Public Resources Code) is designed to reduce losses due to fault displacement. This law requires the State Geologist to delineate special studies zones encompassing active and potentially active faults. Local government must require special studies within these zones before permitting structures for human occupancy. Proposed real estate developments or structures designed for human occupancy within the special study zones shall be approved by the city or county having jurisdiction over such lands pursuant to policies and criteria to be established by the State Mining and Geology Board.

The Uniform Building Code does not recognize fault displacement as a factor to be considered during development, but local ordinances are beginning to be enacted to ameliorate this problem. Los Angeles County was the first local jurisdiction to enact a fault ordinance (Earthquake Fault Ordinance No. 10,362). This ordinance requires the County Engineer to maintain maps showing the location of active faults within the county. A proposal for any structure used for human occupancy must be evaluated in conjunction with the use of these maps. If a proposed building site lies within 50 feet of a known active fault, trenching must be conducted at the site to determine whether an active trace is present. No building may be constructed upon an active fault trace.

Losses from fault displacement tend to be relatively low, but it must be remembered that these do not include the extensive losses due to earthquake shaking. Major losses due to fault displacement have been limited to the San Fernando Valley area where an estimated 200 houses (average value $25,000) and three commercial buildings (estimated value $200,000) were destroyed in 1971 for a total loss of $5,200,000. Structural losses due to fault displacement in the 26 other major earthquakes in California are unknown but were probably small, averaging perhaps $5,000 per event for an additional total of $130,000. Damage to roads, pipelines, canals, and other linear man-made facilities can be significant. Farmers in Kern County spent a substantial but unreported amount of money repairing water systems and re-leveling fields disrupted by displacement on the White Wolf fault in the 1952 Arvin-Tehachapi earthquake, which occurred during the irrigation season.

A further aspect of fault displacement is fault creep, which involves the slow movement along a fault without accompanying significant earthquakes. Damage due to fault creep has been recorded along three faults in the San Francisco Bay Area; the Hayward fault in Hayward, Berkeley and Richmond; the Calaveras fault in Hollister and east of Morgan Hill; and the San Andreas fault south of Hollister. The creep is expressed by the rupture or bending of buildings, irrigation ditches, tunnels, streets, and curbs. Although the structures have been damaged, in all cases they are still in use and, therefore, the losses are small.

The present state of the art is such that active faults can be identified and located through detailed geologic mapping, seismic study, trenching, drilling, and geophysical work. Although this work may be expensive, it is possible to locate most active faults accurately and thereafter guide development so that losses due to fault displacement on known active faults can be virtually eliminated.

Volcanic Hazards

The effects of volcanic eruptions rank with the most devastating natural disasters known to man. An area that has been overwhelmed by the products of an eruption may be totally destroyed, the lives of all who have not escaped lost, buildings destroyed or rendered unusable, water supply systems destroyed or polluted; and, depending on the type of eruption, farmlands converted to sterile, rocky landscapes which may not be productive for decades or even hundreds of years to come.

Volcanoes produce several kinds of products depending upon the composition and properties of the material erupted. However, almost all volcanoes tend to produce similar materials with each eruption. The various types of eruptions are:

1. Peléan eruption. This type of eruption is typified by the 1902 eruption of Mt. Pelée on the island of Martinique in the West Indies. The eruption destroyed the city of St. Pierre with the loss of more than 30,000 lives. The Peléan type of eruption produces lava of high viscosity and is characterized by extreme explosiveness. Its distinguishing feature is a *nuée ardente* or "glowing cloud", a mass of incandescent ash particles so charged with highly heated gas that it resembles a mobile emulsion, yet is dense enough to maintain contact with the ground surface as it rushes down the slopes of the mountain with hurricane force. The upward escape of the molten lava in the central crater is frequently blocked by a plug of solidified lava and explosions break out as horizontal blasts from beneath the plug. It was this type of eruption that produced the devastated area on the northeastern slope of Mt. Lassen during the eruption of May 1915.
2. Lava flows. Eruptions of this type are typical of the Hawaiian volcanos, from which abundant outpourings of fluid lava take place. The contained gases are releases more or less quietly, although fountains of lava may be expelled from the crater and fissures. Lava flows may sweep across the countryside for tens or even hundreds of miles. The 1851–52 eruption of a basalt flow from the base of the cinder cone east of Mt. Lassen is an historic example of this type of volcanic activity (James 1966, p. 303). There is abundant evidence in the geologic record that lava flows have taken place throughout the past in California and can be expected in the future.
3. Cinder cones. This type of eruption is normally contained within a small area. The eruption consists of more or less regular explosions of moderate intensity which throw out pasty, incandescent lava (scoria), accompanied by a vapor cloud. The lava in the crater cools enough to crust over lightly and at regular intervals the pent-up gases escape with mild explosions, hurling out clots of lava and fragments of the crust. Eruptions of this type are commonly associated with lava flows. Although no cinder cones are known to have erupted in California since the arrival of white settlers, numerous fresh cinder cones indicate widespread activity of this type in the past few hundred years.
4. Ash fall. The expulsion of solid fragments is one of the most spectacular phases of some volcanic eruptions. Millions of hot, frothy, dust or sand-sized fragments may be blown miles into the air and then swept away by air currents and dropped many miles from their point of origin. The 1883 eruption of Krakatoa, near Java, was one of the greatest volcanic eruptions of historic time. It is estimated that one cubic mile of material was blown to a height of seventeen miles and that dust from the eruption was carried completely around the earth several times. Dust fell in quantities on ships 1600 miles away three days after the eruption. The intensity of the sun's rays reaching the earth's surface for the year following the eruption were only 87 percent of normal, and the products of this eruption covered more than 135,000,000 square miles of the earth's surface.
5. Volcanic mudflows. Eruptions may be accompanied by the release of large quantities of water which mix with loose volcanic materials to form swiftly moving mudflows. The water is derived from crater or caldera reservoirs or from melting snow or rain formed by the condensation of moist air carried to cooler altitudes by updrafts, and to a limited extent by the condensation of steam released by the volcanic eruption. The rapidly moving mixture of volcanic material and water may form a high-density slurry capable of transporting rocks weighing many tons. On coming to rest, these mudflows harden to form tuff-breccia rock materials.

Most of the products of volcanic eruptions produce damage by the intrinsic heat within their rocks or by covering the works of man beneath their voluminous deposits.

Photo 12. Cerro Negro Volcano, Nicaragua, in eruption. *Photo by James Sorenson, Mark Hurd Aerial Surveys Corp.*

Although the damage caused by volcanic eruptions can be total, their recurrence through time is infrequent enough that man may live between eruptions with relative ease. Known potentially damaging eruptions in California, since the beginning of the Christian era, follow (Chesterman, 1971):

1914–1917	Lava flows, ash falls, and *nuée ardentes* from Mt. Lassen, Shasta County.
1890	Eruptions beneath the surface of Mono Lake, Mono County.
1857	An ash fall from either Mt. Lassen, Shasta County, or Mt. Shasta, Siskiyou County.
1851–52	Formation of Cinder Cone and attendant lava flows east of Mt. Lassen, Shasta County.
1786	Steam and ash from either Mt. Lassen, Shasta County, or Mt. Shasta, Siskiyou County.
±1470	Surface eruption forming the cinder cones and flow of burnt lava flow, Siskiyou County.
±1100–1450	Explosive eruptions at Inyo Crater, Inyo County.
± 900	Extensive eruptions during the formation of pumice deposits, lava flows and obsidian domes at Big Glass Mountain, Siskiyou County.

Volcanic eruptions cannot be controlled, although there have been successful attempts to divert lava flows. Obviously the effects of eruptions should be avoided and this is best achieved through advance warnings of an eruption by means of geophysical monitoring. The two methods that have been most successful are:

1. Seismographs, which can detect earth tremors resulting from the subsurface movement of molten magma into conduits. Major eruptions are commonly preceded by strong, local earthquakes.
2. Tiltmeters, which can detect minute differences in earth inclination. Instrument readings on the Hawaiian volcanos indicate that volcano slopes swell outward before an eruption and collapse inward following an eruption.

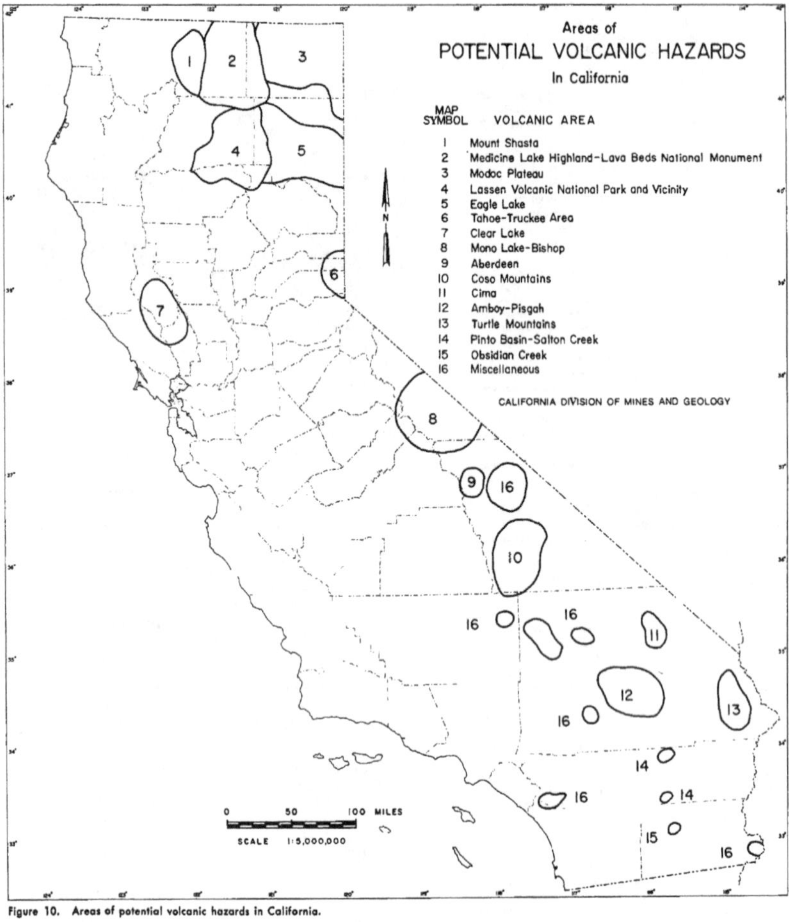

Figure 10. Areas of potential volcanic hazards in California.

Volcanic hazards are studied by geologists of the California Division of Mines and Geology and the U.S. Geological Survey. Priority for these studies is generally lower, however, than that for work on other geologic hazards.

The most probable centers of future volcanic eruptions have been outlined by Chesterman (1971). These areas generally lie along the eastern margin of California, with the greatest concentrations in northeastern California and along the eastern margin of the Sierra Nevada. Figure 10 shows the generalized distribution of potential volcanic hazards in California.

For all of their destructive potential, there have been few losses in California from volcanic eruptions. Those few eruptions that have occurred did so in remote areas. There were some losses resulting from a mudflow from the 1915 eruption of Mt. Lassen. Several farm buildings were destroyed and several persons barely escaped when a wall of mud 12 feet high swept down Lost Creek Canyon (Hill, 1970). Monetary losses probably were no more than a few thousand dollars.

It is not possible to estimate future statewide losses accurately. The sparsity of events in historic time hinders the making of statistical estimates of future events; 30-year losses could range from zero to many millions of dollars, depending upon factors of occurrence, kind, severity, location, and time.

The use of land in the vicinity of volcanoes has greatly increased since the last eruption in 1917 and it is reasonable to assume that the low losses in the past will not be the rule in the future. Property losses would accompany an eruption at any time and if an unexpected eruption occurred during a summer tourist season, loss of life could be high.

The most effective warning system would be obtained by extending the State seismograph system to include all eruption-prone areas. A seismograph has been operating for many years at Mt. Lassen; others should be installed at Mt. Shasta, Lava Beds National Monument, Clear Lake, Mono Lake, and the Salton Sea. As other less populated areas become developed, stations should be added.

In potentially hazardous areas that have not yet been urbanized, zoning or other land use controls can be effective in reducing future losses.

Tsunami Hazards

Tsunamis, or seismic sea waves, are great oceanic waves that are generated by earthquakes, submarine volcanic eruptions or large submarine landslides. The waves are formed in groups having great length from crest to crest and having a long period. In deep ocean areas, wave-lengths may be a hundred miles or more and wave heights, from crest to trough, may be only a few feet. Tsunamis cannot be felt aboard ships in deep water and normally cannot be seen from the air, but intrinsic wave energies are nonetheless impressive. As a tsunami enters shallower waters along coastlines, wave velocity diminishes and wave height increases. If a trough precedes the initial crest, the arrival of a tsunami is heralded by a gradual recession of coastal water; if a crest precedes, there is a rise in water level. Following this are large waves, some of which can crest at heights of more than 100 feet and strike with devastating force (U.S. Coast and Geodetic Survey, 1955). Seiches are similar, but smaller, low-energy waves that form in smaller bodies of water such as lakes and bays.

Tsunamis affect coastal areas and coastal watercourses. Figure 11 shows the distribution of tsunami hazard areas in California. The forces involved are so great that the only positive means of protection is to avoid areas subject to tsunamis. The basic function of the seismic sea-wave warning system administered by the National Oceanic and Atmospheric Administration is to provide warnings of the approach of potentially damaging tsunamis. The system uses seismographs to detect and locate earthquakes; and tide gauges to detect passing tsunami waves. Automatic alarms are triggered when a tsunami is detected. Methods for determining travel times have been improved so that arrival times now can be predicted to within a minute and a half per elapsed hour. Communication links have been established using the network facilities of the Federal Aviation Agency, Defense Communications Agency, National Aeronautics and Space Administration and U.S. Weather Bureau. Warning times vary with distances from the source, but periods of several to many hours usually are available to evacuate populations to safe areas.

The earthquake of 1812 was associated with the largest tsunami ever reported in California. The wave may have reached land elevations of 50 feet at Gaviota, 30 to 35 feet at Santa Barbara, and 15 or more feet at Ventura (Wood and Heck, 1966).

Damage due to tsunamis in California has almost always been greatest at Crescent City in Del Norte County, regardless of points of origin. Wave heights have been recorded as follows:

Date	Point of origin	Wave height at Crescent City
1947	Aleutian Trench	5.9 ft.
1952	Kamchatka	6.8 ft.
1957	Aleutian Islands	4.3 ft.
1960	Chile	10.9 ft.
1964	Alaska	13.0 ft.

The high wave heights at Crescent City perhaps reflect circumstances of exposed coastal location or possibly some unknown peculiarity of bottom topography.

The most damaging tsunami of recent years followed the Alaska earthquake of 1964, and cost the lives of 11 persons at Crescent City. Damage along the California coast was as follows:

Crescent City	$11,000,000
Long Beach	100,000
Los Angeles	275,000
Marin County	1,000,000
Noyo Harbor	1,000,000
Total	$13,375,000

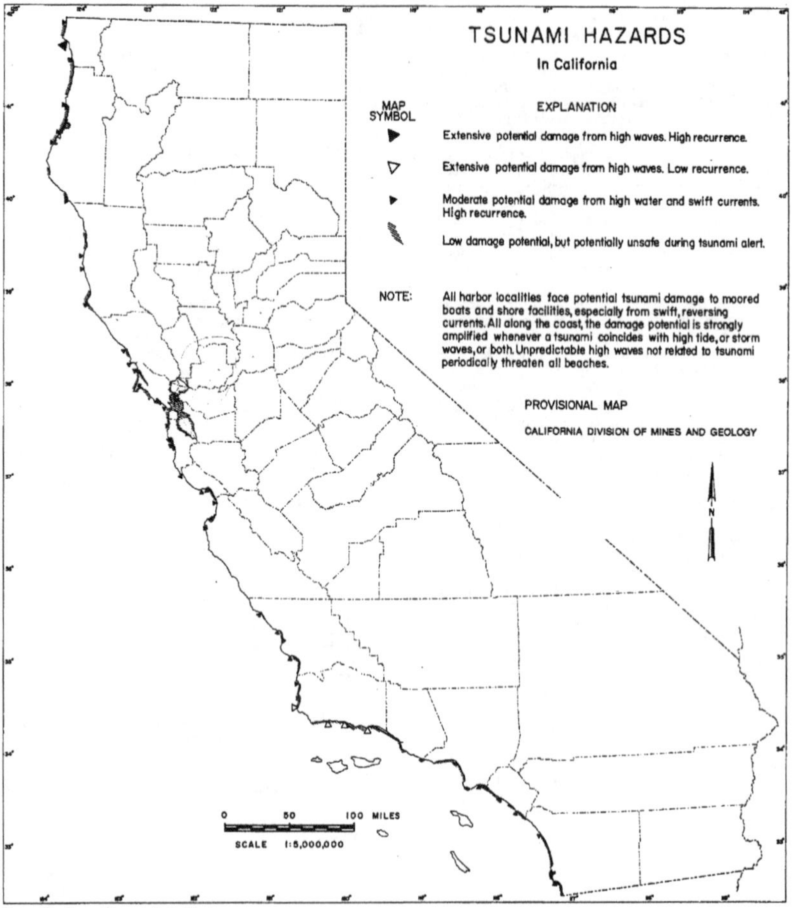

Figure 11. Tsunami hazards in California.

Photo 13. Tsunami damage at Crescent City, 1964. U.S. Army Corps of Engineers photo.

Continued improvement can be expected in the existing warning system, but for the most part the system is adequate to meet present needs. Since it is impossible to control tsunamis, care should be taken to avoid development in areas that have been inundated in the past.

Subsidence*

Subsidence of the land surface, as a result of the activities of man, has been occurring in California for many years. Subsidence can be divided, on the basis of causative mechanisms, into four types: ground-water withdrawal subsidence, oil or gas withdrawal subsidence, hydrocompaction subsidence, and peat oxidation subsidence. The distribution of the four types of subsidence in California is shown in figure 12.

GROUND-WATER WITHDRAWAL SUBSIDENCE

Ground-water withdrawal subsidence is the most extensive and has been the most costly of the four types of subsidence in California. This type of subsidence has been observed only in valley areas underlain by alluvium. These areas are, from north to south, 1) small areas near Arbuckle and Zamora in Colusa and northern Solano counties, 2) an extensive area in the delta of the Sacramento and San Joaquin rivers, 3) the Santa Clara Valley, 4) a very large area in the central San Joaquin Valley, 5) Pleasant Valley in southwestern Fresno County, 6) a large area at the south end of the San Joaquin Valley, 7) Antelope Valley, 8) a large area in southwestern San Bernardino County and eastern Los Angeles County called the La Verne, Chino-Riverside and Bunker Hill-Yucaipa area, 9) the Beverly Hills area, 10) the Watts area, 11) Santa Ana area and 12) the San Jacinto Valley-Hemet area.

Ground surface effects, related to ground-water withdrawal, may take many forms. In tidal areas, flooding by sea water can be a major problem. Changing gradients have seriously affected the carrying capacities of canals, drains, and sewers, and have

* Based on material prepared by William R. Hanson, Woodward-Lundgren & Associates, Oakland.

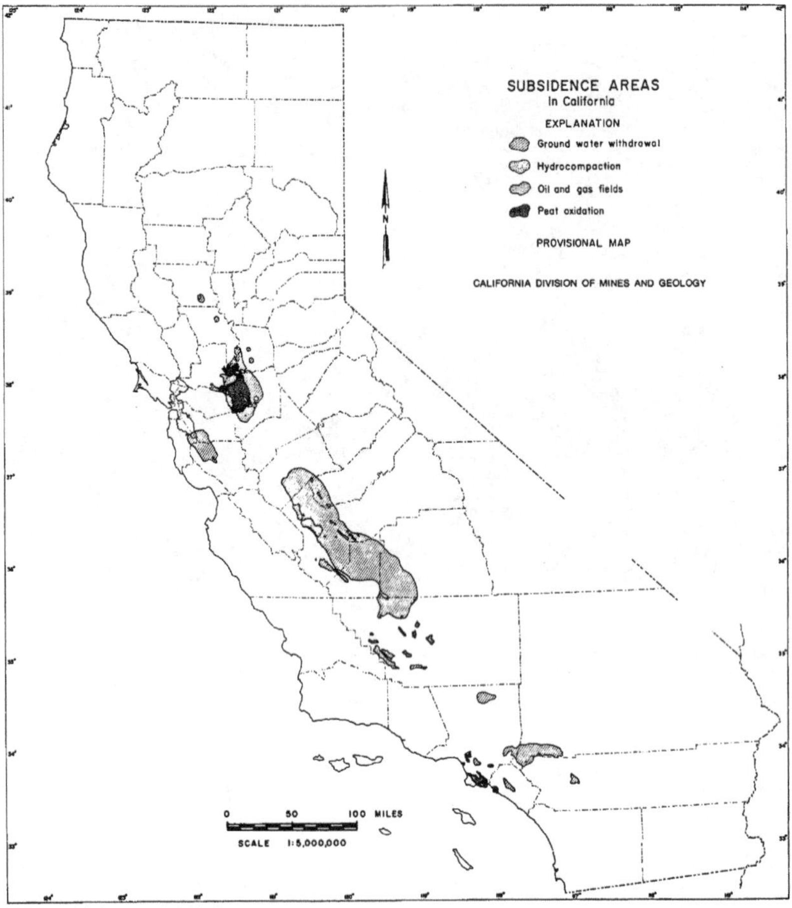

Figure 12. Subsidence areas in California.

Photo 14. Oil withdrawal subsidence at Long Beach for the period 1928 to 1972. Photo by City of Long Beach, Department of Oil Properties.

Photo 15. Hydrocompaction subsidence around a test pit on the west side of the San Joaquin Valley. California Department of Water Resources photo.

changed channel capacities of streams. Compaction of sediments at depth has caused extensive damage to water wells in areas where subsidence has been substantial. Such damage has taken the form of the telescoping, collapse, and shearing of well casings and the protrusion of some casings above land surfaces.

Except for water wells, effects related to groundwater withdrawal subsidence are generally restricted to lengthy surface structures such as canals and pipelines sensitive to slight changes in elevation. Subsidence usually occurs over broad areas and is not normally perceptible at the ground surface unless some means of reference, such as the water level in a canal or the protrusion of a well casing above ground, is available to the observer. Centers of maximum subsidence generally correspond to centers of ground-water withdrawal and to points of maximum decline in water levels. Maximum subsidence also seems to correspond with areas of confined ground water. The magnitude of subsidence depends primarily on the following five factors:

1. The magnitude of water level decline.
2. The thickness of the alluvium tapped by wells.
3. The individual and combined thicknesses and compressibilities of the silt and clay layers within vertical sections tapped by wells.
4. The lengths of time during which water level declines are maintained.
5. The number of occurrences of heavy withdrawals of water in any single area.

In planning with reference to future ground-water withdrawal subsidence, it is important to consider two points: 1) the type of area in which subsidence will occur and, 2) the amount or degree of subsidence which may occur in a particular area. It has been found that the substantial and first-time lowerings of water levels in valley fill alluviums are the primary causes of withdrawal subsidence. Subsidence is worsened in areas of confined ground water and in areas having alluvial beds of compressible silts and clays. Studies of subsidence have been made and are being continued, in a number of basins in the state, by the California Department of Water Resources, the U.S. Geological Survey, and the U.S. Bureau of Reclamation.

In many portions of the state, potentials for subsidence are being studied and estimated by means of determining 1) degrees of ground-water confinement, 2) thicknesses of aquifer systems, 3) individual and total thicknesses of fine-grained beds, 4) compressibility of the fine-grained layers, 5) probable future depth of wells, and 6) probable future decline in ground water levels.

OIL AND GAS WITHDRAWAL SUBSIDENCE

Twenty-two oil and gas fields in California are known to have experienced subsidence. The better documented of these fields are located in the Los Angeles basin where considerable damage has occurred to the works of man. The most dramatic example of subsidence damage has taken place in the Wilmington field near Long Beach.

The area that subsided over the Wilmington field is intensively industrialized and initially was only 5 to 10 feet above sea level. By 1966, subsidence had placed much of the area well below sea level and extensive construction of dikes and raising of dock facilities was required. Surface deformation within the subsidence bowl had caused extensive damage to pipelines, railroad tracks, and buildings.

Surface deformation, associated with oil and gas field operations in California, has manifested itself in the differential subsidence of lands centering on the fields, inwardly directed horizontal displacements, and faulting. Twenty-two fields have experienced differential subsidence, three have experienced horizontal subsidence, and five have experienced faulting (Yerkes and Castle, 1969).

Differential subsidence is the most common and widespread of the surface effects. Subsidence centers over and extends well beyond the producing areas and frequently takes the shape of a bowl. Large subsidence bowls have been documented over the Wilmington field, the Huntington Beach field, the Long Beach field, and the Inglewood field.

Subsidence of the land surface, as a result of the withdrawal of oil and gas, occurs in much the same way as does subsidence in ground-water withdrawal. That is, as pore pressures are reduced in reservoirs by fluid withdrawal, the overburden load is gradually transferred to reservoir rocks and poorly consolidated claystone and shale layers are compacted.

In the case of oil fields, magnitudes of subsidence may be comparable to those found in circumstances of ground-water withdrawal. The world subsidence record is held by the Wilmington oil field where a maximum of 29 feet of subsidence was recorded to 1966, when subsidence was halted at Wilmington by repressurization in conjunction with the secondary recovery of oil. The world record for subsidence may soon pass to the area 40 miles west of Fresno, along the west side of the San Joaquin Valley, where a maximum of 28 feet of ground-water subsidence was recorded by 1969.

Subsidence due to gas withdrawal alone apparently does not reach magnitudes comparable to oil withdrawal subsidence. Perhaps for this reason subsidence due to gas withdrawal is not widely recognized, and if subsidence is detected over a gas field, separation from other types of subsidence, which may be going on concurrently, may be difficult.

In a study of the Inglewood oil field, Castle, Yerkes, and Riley (1969) discovered an apparent linear relationship between net liquid production and subsidence in the Baldwin Hills area. Their findings show promise in the estimating of future subsidence in areas of oil and gas withdrawals. In their studies, the linear relationship between net liquid production and subsidence were found to be valid in three Venezuelan fields, in the Wilmington oil field during primary production stages, and in the Huntington Beach oil field. Success with the relationship in these fields suggests that this linearity may be a general phenomenon applicable for prediction in other oil fields.

HYDROCOMPACTION SUBSIDENCE

Hydrocompaction is a phenomenon most common in desert environments, but it has been noticed in some of the semi-arid regions in southern California (Antelope Valley and upper Santa Clara Valley). It has been reported on certain alluvial fans along the western side of the San Joaquin Valley. Hydrocompaction occurs above zones of saturation, and usually occurs within a few hundred feet of the land surface. For this reason, it is also referred to as "shallow subsidence" in contrast to the "deep subsidence" associated with oil, gas, and ground-water withdrawals.

Hydrocompaction occurs when certain open-textured soils lose their strength and consolidate under their own weight. Consolidation and subsidence usually occur when these soils become saturated with water for the first time.

Hydrocompaction is a problem to the works of man because of the abruptness and short distances over which subsidence occurs. A common result is severe ground surface cracking. Hydrocompaction has destroyed or damaged ditches, canals, roads, pipelines, electric transmission towers, and buildings. In some areas, the irrigation of crops has been made difficult. In California, about 124 square miles of land surface has subsided or probably would subside if irrigated; subsidence of 3 to 5 feet is common and more than 10 feet of subsidence has been recorded in some small areas.

Hydrocompaction subsidence along the western side of the San Joaquin has been intensively studied primarily because of its effect on the many canals that pass through the area. The results of these studies in California comprise virtually all that is presently known of the phenomenon.

Along the west side of the San Joaquin Valley, the alluvial fan deposits occur as mudflows, water-laid sediments, or as types intermediate between the two. Intermediate and mudflow fans are most commonly associated with subsidence, whereas water-laid sediments tend to be nonsubsiding.

Mudflows usually originate during periods of high intensity rainfall. As a mudflow travels valleyward, it becomes increasingly desiccated both through evaporation and through the dissemination of runoff water into surrounding dry soils. Desiccation and turbulent flow result in the low unit weight and the open-textured characteristics of mudflow soils. Soil strengths in flow materials are, furthermore, usually greatly diminished because of high clay and silt compositions.

When water is later applied, either by irrigation or from canal leakage to soils susceptible to hydrocompaction, the soils in the wetted areas collapse. Collapse occurs as the clay bonding and cohesive strengths in the soils surrounding the voids are weakened by water percolating through the deposit for the first time. The amount of subsidence is dependent mainly on overburden loads, soil shear strengths, natural moisture conditions, and the amount and type of clay in the deposits.

In attempting to remedy hydrocompaction problems encountered during construction of the California Aqueduct, the California Department of Water Resources employed a remedial procedure involving the ponding of water along the aqueduct route. The infiltration of ponded water saturated underlying sediments and allowed these to consolidate until all significant subsidence had taken place. Construction of the aqueduct then proceeded.

This same technique could be used prior to most construction in areas of potential hydrocompaction, but could be costly, and in desert areas where water is a premium resource, might not be feasible. Experienced geologists can recognize areas of potential hydrocompaction and soils engineers can recommend remedial measures.

PEAT OXIDATION SUBSIDENCE

The delta of the Sacramento and San Joaquin Rivers, in the central portion of the Great Valley, is believed to comprise the second largest continuous body of peat lands in the United States, exceeded only by the Everglades in Florida. The delta consists of a number of islands, surrounded by a network of waterways. The reclamation of swamp and island areas has led to an unusual subsidence problem in the delta.

Prior to reclamation and development, the surface of the delta was at or slightly above sea level and was inundated only at periods of high tide or at times of river flood stage. Much of the swamp was covered by a dense growth of tules with fringes of willows and other woody plants along the slightly higher stream banks.

The steps in the delta reclamation process consisted of:

1. The construction of levees around each of the islands.
2. The burning of the dry tules.
3. The construction of main drainage ditches and pumping systems.
4. The plowing and cultivation of the delta surface to depths of 2 feet when soils become dry.

Peat deposits in the delta range in thickness from a few inches to more than 40 feet. In the central delta, thicknesses vary between 20 and 40 feet. Subsidence is greatest at the centers of the individual islands in the delta and with time many islands have taken on bowl shapes. The average cumulative subsidence to 1952 appears to have ranged from 11 to 14 feet.

Subsidence in peat soils is the result of several factors operating together. These factors include: oxidation of the peat, burning, wind erosion, shrinkage from drying, and compaction by tillage machinery. Of these five factors, oxidation of the peat seems to be the single most important factor, and for this reason, the phenomenon has been called "peat oxidation subsidence".

In their virgin condition, the delta soils were almost completely submerged, and oxidation either did not occur or was greatly retarded. Oxidation is most likely the result of the action of aerobic bacteria above the water table. Other factors such as compaction by tillage machinery, shrinkage by drying, burning, and wind erosion seem to be minor.

It seems that subsidence will continue in the delta as long as the water table is maintained at a position lower than ground surface. As drainage goes hand in hand with cultivation, it is unlikely that subsidence will stop until the peat has been completely oxidized. Greater subsidence of the individual islands will place increasing loads on the levees that keep the surrounding water from inundating lower areas. Weir (1950) points out that once a breach in the levee occurs and the islands flood, it may not always be economically feasible to re-drain flooded areas. As an example, Weir points to Frank's Tract which contains more than 3,000 acres of flooded delta lands. Reclamation and drainage costs are prohibitively high and the tract will probably remain unreclaimed and flooded for many years to come.

The delta of the Sacramento-San Joaquin Rivers is a unique area in California in which two kinds of subsidence contribute to the total subsidence picture. Ground-water withdrawal subsidence is occurring in addition to that caused by peat oxidation. To differentiate those portions due to each type of subsidence is a difficult matter, however, and no worker in the field has attempted to do this to date. The techniques developed by the U.S. Geological Survey could probably be applied here to separate amounts attributable to each type of subsidence, but until that is done, predictions of projected subsidence will not be feasible.

Subsidence of various kinds is studied by geologists in agencies concerned with either the causes or the results of subsidence. Ground water and oil and gas withdrawal subsidence is studied by the U.S. Geological Survey, the California Department of Water Resources, and the California Division of Oil and Gas. Hydrocompaction subsidence is studied by the U.S. Geological Survey, the California Department of Water Resources, and the U.S. Bureau of Reclamation. Peat oxidation subsidence is closely related to agricultural use and as a result has been studied by the California Agricultural Station, at Berkeley.

The California Division of Oil and Gas directly controls subsidence due to the withdrawal of oil and gas; additional control is provided in some southern California areas by local petroleum production administrations. Most other types of subsidence are not regulated by law. Subsidence due to ground-water withdrawals is variable, and is loosely controlled by local water conservation districts. Peat oxidation subsidence is not controlled in any way at present.

Comprehensive data on the total losses due to subsidence are not available but some examples can be cited. Total subsidence losses in the city of Long Beach have been estimated at $100,000,000 and have involved extensive damages to buildings, harbor structures, and pipelines. The Baldwin Hills Reservoir failure in Los Angeles is thought by some to have been caused by subsidence; direct losses were five lives and $15,000,000 property damage.

Hydrocompaction on the west side of the San Joaquin Valley required special consideration during construction of the California Aqueduct. Engineering costs were $2,700,000 and special ground preparation costs were nearly $13,000,000. The Delta-Mendota Canal was built without knowledge of the problem and later subsidence of certain portions of the canal required the spending of unknown but large amounts of money for repair.

Subsidence due to the withdrawals of water, oil and gas can be slowed or stopped by reservoir repressurization. This is done by injecting water, under high pressure, into zones of reservoir depletion. Surveillance of basins being pumped should continue so that any vertical movements taking place can be detected and corrected.

Hydrocompaction may be much more common than is generally suspected because so little development has taken place in desert areas. Any future development in desert areas should, however, consider the possibilities of the occurrence of hydrocompaction.

Subsidence is a problem to the works of man only as it occurs after these works are constructed. It is therefore important to recognize areas where potentials for subsidence may exist and to recognize also the possible magnitude of effects at the land surface before development is contemplated.

Section 4

Recommendations for Reducing Geologic Hazards Losses in California

General S[illegible]

Section 3 of this report d[illegible]
geologic problems that thre[illegible]
logic nature of each problem[illegible]
by severity levels; history o[illegible]
measures for reducing the l[illegible]
agencies that deal with the[illegible]
of the art in coping with ea[illegible]
in effect, a capsule inventor[illegible]
the problems.

Section 4 lists, in broad co[illegible]
that can be implemented t[illegible]
sulting from each geologic p[illegible]
grams constitute the recomm[illegible]
Geology Master Plan for C[illegible]
mended programs are of two k[illegible]
to improve the state of the ar[illegible]
greater capabilities for dealing[illegible]
logic problems on both the [illegible]
technical levels; and those tha[illegible]
application of present state-o[illegible]
reduce losses further. Many of[illegible]
grams are presently active t[illegible]
to be expanded or accelerated[illegible]
stituted.

The recommended action[illegible]
types of objectives, arrang[illegible]
sequence relative to the expec[illegible]
ticular geologic hazard events[illegible]

1. Avoid or prevent damage from[illegible] the nature and location of po[illegible] to control these events, and gu[illegible] from hazardous areas in which[illegible] the hazards.
2. Minimize unavoidable or unprev[illegible] thorough analysis of the poss[illegible] design, then provide safe desig[illegible] tenance practices by competent [illegible]
3. Take emergency action to save[illegible] or immediately following an [illegible]
4. Take longer-range recovery act[illegible] event, to study its lessons, rebu[illegible] uild.

Recommended action progr[illegible]
enced for each of the 10 urban[illegible]
gether with recommendations[illegible]
tions should implement each p[illegible]

Priorities—as to which prob[illegible]
ered first, in which localities a[illegible]
first, which loss-reducing acti[illegible]
first, or which action organizati[illegible]
initiate its programs—are conside[illegible]

Table 4, "Loss-reduction fun[illegible]
main functions that can and sho[illegible]
reduce losses from geologic proble[illegible]
programs recommended for speci[illegible]
in the pages following table 4 [illegible]

RECOMMENDATIONS FOR REDUCING GEOLOGIC HAZARDS LOSSES IN CALIFORNIA

General Statement

Section 3 of this report describes the ten principal geologic problems that threaten California: the geologic nature of each problem; statewide distribution, by severity levels; history of losses; the most effective measures for reducing the losses from problems; the agencies that deal with the problem; and the state of the art in coping with each problem. Section 3 is, in effect, a capsule inventory of what we know about the problems.

Section 4 lists, in broad form, the action programs that can be implemented to reduce future losses resulting from each geologic problem. These action programs constitute the recommendations of the Urban Geology Master Plan for California. The recommended programs are of two kinds: those that propose to improve the state of the art and to develop new and greater capabilities for dealing with California's geologic problems on both the technical and the nontechnical levels; and those that propose to expand the application of present state-of-the-art procedures to reduce losses further. Many of the recommended programs are presently active to some degree, but need to be expanded or accelerated; others need to be instituted.

The recommended actions involve four broad types of objectives, arranged roughly by time-sequence relative to the expected occurrence of particular geologic hazard events:

1. Avoid or prevent damage from future events by assessing the nature and location of probable events, taking steps to control those events, and guiding human activities away from hazardous areas in which it is not feasible to correct the hazards.
2. Minimize unavoidable or unpreventable losses by requiring thorough analysis of the geologic environment prior to design, then provide safe design, construction, and maintenance practices by adequate codes and ordinances.
3. Take emergency action to save lives and property during or immediately following any particular disastrous event.
4. Take longer-range recovery action following a particular event, to study its lessons, reestablish normal life, and rebuild.

Recommended action programs are listed or referenced for each of the 10 urban geologic problems, together with recommendations as to which organizations should implement each program.

Priorities—as to which problem should be considered first, in which localities actions should be started first, which loss-reducing actions should be initiated first, or which action organization should act first to initiate its programs—are considered in Section 5.

Table 4, "Loss-reduction functions", lists the seven main functions that can and should be performed to reduce losses from geologic problems. All of the action programs recommended for specific geologic problems in the pages following table 4 fall within these seven functions. The recommended actions are presented by problem, in the order given in table 4.

The loss-reduction functions in table 4 and the recommendations that follow are not equally important in reducing losses from each of the 10 geologic problems: a given function may apply only indirectly to certain geologic problems, or it may be adequately performed now.

Loss-reduction functions cannot be compared to each other in importance for reducing the losses from any single geologic problem. The functions are basically sequential in application, like links in a chain of operation: none does the whole job itself, yet none can be neglected entirely.

The variability of importance of the functions within and between the several geologic problems is apparent from the number and type of programs that are recommended within each function's heading, problem by problem.

This classification of loss-reduction programs repeatedly emphasizes two separate types of actions that are necessary before a recommended function is indeed accomplished:

1. DEVELOP CAPABILITY:
   Learn how to carry out the needed program. Develop the capability or improve the state-of-the-art, and develop or evolve a standard procedure for accomplishing the program. This capability must be made available to those responsible for doing the job.
2. DO THE JOB:
   Properly apply the capability to avoid, prevent, or correct the problem.

The need for this obvious two-step approach is exemplified in the recommendations to produce consistent and complete socio-economic analysis information for each geological problem. First, to develop needed capability, a standard terminology needs to be devised, and a standard format developed for collecting and recording the needed kinds of data, in terms of the units to be used; a standard procedure needs to be devised designating sources to be canvassed and organizations responsible for collecting, collating, and storing the information. Otherwise the record will continue to be made up of fragmentary data about various kinds of losses, which may otherwise be combined in unknown ways with other loss (or loss-reduction) data, and may contain unexpressed assumptions and incompatible units which are incomplete or overlapping in some time-spans or localities. This procedure should be developed with broad participation so as to be generally acceptable, and then made available to all concerned.

Second, the many agencies responsible under the developed procedure must effectively perform the indicated tasks to collect the socio-economic data in the accepted manner.

Table 4. Loss-reduction functions.

A. DATA FUNCTIONS
1. Research programs to gather, prepare, and interpret data.
2. Information dissemination.

B. PLANNING FUNCTIONS
1. Land-use planning.
2. Recovery planning.

C. ENGINEERING FUNCTIONS
1. Planning and design.
2. Construction.

D. ENABLING FUNCTIONS
1. Political and administrative action.
   a. Authority, policy guidance, action dates.
   b. Resources (funds, manpower) to conduct action programs.
2. Coordination and operational guidance (e.g., criteria, model language).

E. ENFORCEMENT FUNCTIONS
1. Governing body and administrative review and management.
2. Operational inspection and enforcement.

F. EMERGENCY-ACTION FUNCTIONS
1. Overall coordination, definition, and guidance.
2. Contingency planning, preparation, and testing.
3. Response.
4. Post-disaster review.

G. OVERALL COGNIZANCE AND COORDINATION FUNCTIONS
1. Monitor progress of loss-reduction measures and techniques.
2. Provide overall coordination mechanism.

Recommended Programs

The following section presents the action programs recommended for immediate implementation to reduce losses from the ten geologic problems considered in the Urban Geology Master Plan project. Collectively, these recommendations constitute the principal end product of the California Urban Geology Master Plan.

The ten geologic problems are arranged in descending order of potential total dollar loss in the state, including dollar-equivalent life-loss, property damage, and intangible losses, from 1970 to the year 2000 if no change is made in the type and level of loss-reduction measures being taken in 1972. (See table 1, in Section 1.) To the extent the amount of potential loss represents the potential benefit if loss-reduction measures could be 100 percent successful, this ranking represents one approach to an order of priority for implementing Urban Geology Master Plan recommendations.

The recommended programs are classified according to the outline presented in table 4. Detail varies from heading to heading and between geologic hazards, according to the nature of the hazard and the applicability or effectiveness of the several types of recommendations.

The numbers in parentheses following each recommended program indicate:

(1) This is a new program.

(2) This is an enlargement of a program now active in some places or to some degree in California; it should be expanded in scope, or extended to other jurisdictions, or accelerated to completion, above its 1972 levels by at least 100 percent.

(3) This represents a continuation of a program now active, at about its 1972 scope, coverage, and emphasis.

Recommendations in bold-face type are the **Major Recommendations** of the Urban Geology Master Plan—those programs that stand to produce the largest amount of loss reduction in each problem if pursued vigorously.

Abbreviations Used in This Section

STATE AGENCIES

CDF	California Division of Forestry (in Department of Conservation)
CDH	California Division of Highways (in Department of Public Works)
CDMG	California Division of Mines and Geology (in Department of Conservation)
CDOG	California Division of Oil and Gas (in Department of Conservation)
CIR	California Council on Intergovernmental Relations
DC	California Department of Conservation
DI	California Department of Insurance
DGS	California Department of General Services
DHCD	California Department of Housing and Community Development
DNOD	California Department of Navigation and Ocean Development
DPR	California Department of Parks and Recreation
DPW	California Department of Public Works
DRE	California Department of Real Estate
DVA	California Department of Veterans Affairs
DWR	California Department of Water Resources
GEC	California Governor's Earthquake Council
JCSS	Joint Committee on Seismic Safety of the California Legislature
MGB	State Mining and Geology Board
OAC	California Office of Architecture and Construction (in Department of General Services)
OES	California Office of Emergency Services
OIM	Office of Intergovernmental Management
OPR	California Office of Planning and Research
SLD	California State Lands Division

FEDERAL AGENCIES

BLM	U.S. Bureau of Land Management
DCPA	U.S. Defense Civil Preparedness Agency
EPA	U.S. Environmental Protection Agency
FHA	U.S. Federal Housing Administration (in Department of Housing and Urban Development)
FIA	U.S. Federal Insurance Administration (in Department of Housing and Urban Development)
HUD	U.S. Department of Housing and Urban Development
NASA	U.S. National Aeronautics and Space Administration
NOAA	U.S. National Oceanic and Atmospheric Administration
NSF	U.S. National Science Foundation
OEP	U.S. Office of Emergency Preparedness
ONR	U.S. Office of Naval Research
SCS	U.S. Soil Conservation Service
USBR	U.S. Bureau of Reclamation
USCE	U.S. Corps of Engineers (in Department of Defense)
USCG	U.S. Coast Guard
USDA	U.S. Department of Agriculture
USFS	U.S. Forest Service
USGS	U.S. Geological Survey

LOCAL GOVERNMENT AND PRIVATE SECTOR ORGANIZATIONS

AEG	Association of Engineering Geologists
AIA	American institute of Architects
AIME	American Institute of Mining, Metallurgical, and Petroleum Engineers
AIP	American Institute of Planners
ASCE	American Society of Civil Engineers
CSAC	County Supervisors Association of California
CSLL	California Savings and Loan League
DWP	Los Angeles City Department of Water and Power
FAIR	Fair Access to Insurance Requirements
ICBO	International Council of Building Officials
LCC	League of California Cities
MWD	(Los Angeles Area) Metropolitan Water District
PG&E	Pacific Gas and Electric Company
SCE	Southern California Edison Company
SEAOC	Structural Engineers Association of California

Loss-Reduction Programs

I. EARTHQUAKE SHAKING

The Governor's Earthquake Council has recommended a comprehensive program to reduce losses from seismic events in "First Report of the Governor's Earthquake Council, November 21, 1972".

The Joint Committee on Seismic Safety of the California Legislature is conducting various investigations and has issued several progress reports directed primarily to possible legislative actions to reduce losses from seismic events. A number of pieces of seismic safety legislation were passed in 1971 and 1972 reflecting the Joint Committee's work, and more are expected to be enacted in 1973 and future years. The final Joint Committee report is due July 1, 1974.

Rather than duplicate the recommendations of these organizations, the Urban Geology Master Plan refers to the above publications and endorses their recommendations.

One additional recommendation of the Urban Geology Master Plan is to extend the scope of the successor body (Governor's Earthquake Council Recommendation 26 in the *First Report*, page 55) to consider, in addition to seismic hazards, all the other geologic problems covered in this report except loss of mineral resources and flooding.

Recommended Programs	Recommended Agencies*
A–F. (Not applicable)	
G. OVERALL COGNIZANCE AND COORDINATION FUNCTIONS	
Extend scope of successor body to GEC and of JCSS after June 30, 1974 (Recommendation 26 in GEC, 1972, page 55) to provide continuing cognizance over loss-reduction programs for all geologic problems except loss of mineral resources and flooding.[1]	(body to be established)

[1] Essentially a new program

* = Lead or co-lead agency.

Recommended Programs	Recommended Agencies
II. LOSS OF MINERAL RESOURCES (DUE TO URBANIZATION)	
A. DATA FUNCTIONS	
1. Research programs to develop data on mineral deposits.	
a. Geologic processes that cause mineral deposits to form where they are. (Not applicable to loss-reduction.)	
b. Distribution of mineral resources.	
Review, update, and improve (wherever warranted and feasible) maps and descriptions of all known deposits of useful or potentially useful minerals within 100 miles (or commercial haul distance if shorter) of urban areas throughout California. Include all undepleted deposits, whether formerly, currently, or potentially active, regardless of their stage of development or value of past production, if any. Include metals, industrial mineral substances, and mineral fuels.	CDMG*, CDOG, USBM, USGS, County geologists (consultants), Mining associations
i. Statewide scale: (1:250,000–1:1,000,000)[3]	CDMG*, USGS
ii. County/Regional scale: (1:62,500–1:125,000)[2]	CDMG*, USGS
iii. Detail or quadrangle scale: (1:12,000–1:24,000) for urban area deposits, only[2]	CDMG*, Counties, Cities
c. Develop socio-economic information and analyses.	
i. Establish a standard procedure for gathering, collating, and reporting data on the economic and social costs of mineral deposit loss problems—including both loss and loss-reduction costs. The aim is to enable the systematic collection of all pertinent data as it is available, in consistent form so that information collected at different times and places can be correlated and used in statewide compilations and analyses.[1]	CDMG, USBM*, Universities
ii. For every urban region in California and for those outlying regions that have mineral resources serving urban areas, complete a standard economic analysis report, including demand projections, on the problem (or potential problem) of loss of mineral deposits per procedure established under recommendation A-1-c-i.[2]	CDMG, Regional planning agencies, Counties*, Cities
d. Develop research information on engineering problems associated with loss of mineral resources.	
Determine probabilities or limitations of possible development of each mineral (or mining) district, considering limits of valuable material, and removal problems. Consider also forecasts of market demand and any potential engineering problems facing removal of the valuable materials.[2]	CDMG, USBM*, USGS, Mining associations, Counties
e. Case-study projects: Conduct research study of major cases where mineral resources have been lost, or threatened to be lost, due to urbanization processes (e.g., one study in southern California area, one in San Francisco Bay area).	CDMG*, USBM, Minerals industry, City and county, planning departments
2. Information-dissemination programs.	
a. General public information program. Prepare and distribute basic educational materials about the economic, environmental, and social relationships of mineral resources to urban development.	CDMG*, USBM, USGS, Minerals industry
b. Information clearinghouse and data-bank program.	

[1] Essentially a new program
[2] Expansion of 1972 programs
[3] Continue program at 1972 level

* = Lead or co-lead agency.
Bold-face type = Major recommendation of Urban Geology Master Plan

Recommended Programs	Recommended Agencies
i. Continue to serve as clearinghouse and provide data bank service for all information on California mineral resources.[2]	CDMG*, USBM
ii. Expand the types of mineral resource information covered in the data bank to include those recommended in this section.[2]	CDMG*, USBM, USGS
B. PLANNING FUNCTIONS	
1. Land-use planning.	
a. Produce publication describing problems of mineral deposit loss due to blocking of access before the valuable materials can be removed, and the implications of this problem for land-use planning and public policy.[1]	CDMG*, USBM, USGS, AIP, CIR, OPR
b. **Adopt practice of using mineral resource information in determining land-use capability and in the land-use planning, zoning, and permitting procedures of local governments and land-custody agencies. Strengthen mineral resources aspects of conservation elements in general plans, and emphasize their application.**[2]	City and county planning* departments Land-custody agencies: BLM, USBR, DPR, SLD
2. Recovery planning. Apply long-range concepts of conservation, reclamation, and reuse of mineral resource lands in long-range community and land-custody planning procedures.[2]	CDMG, USBM, City and county planning departments * Land-custody agencies, BLM, USBR, SLD
C. ENGINEERING FUNCTIONS	
Improve quarrying and mining procedures to enable the removal of mineral materials within the urban environment with minimum adverse effects. Also improve mining procedures to facilitate long-range policies of multiple sequential uses of mineral deposit lands.[2]	USBM*, CDMG, Minerals industry— firms and associations, Universities, Cities, Counties, AIME
D. ENABLING FUNCTIONS	
1. Political and administrative actions.	
a. Provide authority, policy, and guidance.	
i. **Adopt strengthened conservation element of general plans, incorporating long-range approach to mineral resource utilization.**[3]	City councils, Boards of Supervisors
ii. **Adopt mineral resources zoning ordinance and procedures and practices for making it effective.**[2]	City councils, Boards of Supervisors
b. **Provide resources (funds and manpower) to enable effective administration of the strengthened mineral resources element in the general plan and the mineral resources zoning ordinance.**	City councils, Boards of Supervisors
2. Coordination and operational guidance.	
a. Develop and make information available to land-use planners, zoning administrators, and mineral producers, on proven techniques for developing and extracting mineral deposits in urban areas, applying available geotechnical and socio-economic information about mineral deposits. The aim is to minimize undesirable consequences to the physical, economic and social environment, both immediate and long-range, of mining and quarrying operations. Include considerations of designing the quarry development plan, and managing the long-range reclamation of depleted sites so they will be suitable for high-demand urban uses.[2]	CDMG, USBM, AIP, AEG, Cities, Counties, CSAC*, LCC
b. Establish guidelines, and produce model language for effective conservation element of the general plan that properly treats problems	CIR*, OPR

[1] Essentially a new program
[2] Expansion of 1972 programs
[3] Continue program at 1972 level

* = Lead or co-lead agency
Bold-face type = Major recommendation of Urban Geology Master Plan

of mineral resource conservation; also suggestions for effective administration of that element.[2]	CDMG, AIP, Cities, Counties
c. Provide model of mineral recovery zone ordinance (cf. Riverside County's MR zone), and guidelines for administering it effectively.[2]	CDMG, AIP, CIR*, OPR, Cities, Counties
d. Produce case-studies or other guidance for applying mineral resource information in environmental impact considerations.[2]	CIR, OPR*, CDMG, Cities, Counties

E. ENFORCEMENT FUNCTIONS (Not applicable)

F. EMERGENCY ACTION FUNCTIONS (Not applicable)

G. OVERALL COGNIZANCE AND COORDINATION FUNCTIONS

1. Make periodic evaluation of progress on recommendations in this section and publish annual status reports.[1]	CDMG*, OPR

III. LANDSLIDING

A. DATA FUNCTIONS

1. Research programs to develop data on landsliding.	
a. Research into geologic and other natural processes and conditions that cause or relate to slope stability and landslide movement and their interrelationships.	CDMG*, USGS*, Universities, AEG, DWR, USBM, CDH
i. Develop state of the art, including new instrumentation, to enable analysis of old landslides as to their history and date(s) of prior movement, and their propensity for renewed movements.[1]	USGS*, CDMG*, Universities, DWR, CDH
ii. Develop and improve the state of the art and inexpensive instruments for predicting and detecting incipient renewed movement in known landslides for warning purposes.[1]	Private sector*, Universities, CDH, DWR
iii. Devise workable procedure and criteria to determine the relative stability of slopes. The criteria must be applicable in the field, and should relate the stability characteristics to the uses to which the area can be put.[2]	CDMG*, USGS*, AEG, Cities, Counties
b. Evaluate the varying degrees of slope instability in the urban areas of California.	
i. Compilation (statewide) scale program (1: 250,000–1: 1,000,000).[1]	CDMG*, USGS
ii. County/regional scale program (1:62,500–1:125,000).[1]	CDMG*, USGS, County consultants
iii. Detail or quadrangle scale program (1: 12,000–1: 24,000).[2]	CDMG*, USGS*, Cities, Counties, Consultants
iv. Project-scale mapping for land-use permit decisions or construction purposes (1: 1200–1: 12,000).[2]	Consultants for local governments or developers
c. Develop socio-economic information and analyses.	
i. Establish standard procedure for gathering and compiling figures on landslide damage loss and costs of remedial efforts, for accurate and comparable statistics; devise a form that can be used and compiled statewide, and designate an information clearinghouse.[1]	ICBO,* AEG, ASCE, LCC, CSAC, OES, SEAOC, DI, CIR

[1] Essentially a new program
[2] Expansion of 1972 programs

* = Lead or co-lead agency
Bold-face type = Major recommendation of Urban Geology Master Plan

Recommended Programs	Recommended Agencies
ii. For every reportable landslide occurrence, complete a standard report for permanent record and clearinghouse use.[1]	City and county agencies and/or officials
d. Perform engineering response research.	
i. Investigate behavior of surficial materials at proposed construction sites to determine safe design of foundation and structure. Consider effects of site-preparation work and control accordingly.[2]	Consultant for local government site-approval section, Consultant for builder, Universities, AEG, ASCE
ii. Investigate design and construction standards for foundation and structure to be built at any proposed site, relative to the expectable stability of the geologic setting.[2]	Local government site-approval section, Consultant for builder
e. Event-study opportunities.	
i. Whenever a landslide moves significantly, or damages a foundation or structure, conduct detailed study of the geologic materials and, if present, foundations and structures. Make information on results of studies readily available.[2]	CDMG*, USGS*, City and county building officials, Clearinghouse
ii. During any post-earthquake investigation, search immediately for incipient landslides that may be triggered by aftershocks.[2]	CDMG*, USGS, City and county personnel
2. Information-dissemination programs.	
a. General public information program. Prepare and distribute basic educational materials about landsliding in general, emphasizing local and regional applications, and what the homeowner should know and do about landslides, both before and after they occur.[2]	CDMG*, USGS, CSLL, DI, AEG, ASCE, DRE*, FHA
b. Information clearinghouse and data-bank program. Gather, store and disseminate all pertinent information on landsliding.[1]	CDMG*, USGS
B. PLANNING FUNCTIONS	
1. Land-use planning programs.	
Develop procedures and pursue practice of incorporating landslide and slope-stability information into procedures used to determine land-use capability, and apply in local government and land-custody agency land-use planning procedures (e.g., strengthen safety element and emphasize its application).[2]	AIP, LCC, CSAC, CIR*, OPR, CDMG, AEG, USGS, ASCE, City and county planning departments, Land-custody agencies (e.g., BLM, USFS, DPW, DPR, SLD, DGS, CDF)
2.. Recovery planning programs. Conduct study to evaluate public and private landslide-insurance programs in California, considering combination with insurance for all natural disaster losses; recommend alternatives for improvement.[1]	DI*, FIA*, DWR (Insurance coordinator), DRE, FAIR, DHCD, JCSS, DVA, FHA, Insurance associations
C. ENGINEERING FUNCTIONS	
In planning and designing public works structures, adopt standard procedure of considering threat of landslide, and modify structure as necessary.[3]	Dam-building agencies (USCE, DWR, BLM, USBR, USFS), Road-building agencies (DPW)

[1] Essentially a new program
[2] Expansion of 1972 programs
[3] Continue program at 1972 level

* = Lead or co-lead agency.
Bold-face type = Major recommendation of Urban Geology Master Plan

Recommended Programs	Recommended Agencies
D. ENABLING FUNCTIONS	
1. Political and administrative actions.	
a. Provide authority, policy guidance.	
i. Adopt strengthened safety and seismic safety elements in general plan, incorporating improved landslide considerations.[2]	City councils, Boards of Supervisors
ii. Adopt latest, improved version of grading ordinance (see A-4-a, b).[2]	City councils, Boards of Supervisors
b. Provide funds and staff to make land-use plan effective, and to enable zoning and grading ordinances to be enforced.[2]	City councils, Boards of Supervisors
2. Coordinated, informational guidance.	
a. Produce model safety element for local general plans, especially as it deals with slope-stability problems.[1]	**CIR*, OPR, CDMG, CSAC, LCC, AEG**
b. Periodically update model grading ordinance, especially as it deals with landslide problems, with guidance on how it can be applied effectively, including case studies of successful grading ordinance enforcement practice.[2]	**ICBO*, CDMG, CIR, CSAC, LCC, AEG, ASCE**
c. Assemble and distribute case-studies, and other informational materials on applications of landslide information in environmental impact considerations, including case studies of successful practice.[2]	USGS, CDMG, OPR*, AEG, ASCE, OIM, CIR
d. Produce interpretive publication, alerting and orienting planners and and administrators to the significance and usefulness of geotechnical information on landsliding and on the engineering response, and on its application in land-use planning and decision making.[1]	CDMG*, USGS, AEG, ASCE
E. ENFORCEMENT FUNCTIONS	
1. Administrative follow-through; management control.	
a. Strengthen local government programs and capabilities for effective inspections of grading practices, including requirement of pre-construction geological study of slope stability conditions at site.[2]	City councils, Boards of Supervisors
b. Maintain integrity of zoning and grading ordinances (as they apply to landsliding) in arriving at individual land-use decisions.[2]	City councils, Boards of Supervisors, Appeals Boards
2. Conduct on-site inspections of building sites as necessary to assure that the various actions to prevent damage from landsliding are properly taken, as required by safety regulations, and zoning and grading ordinances.[2]	City and county grading inspectors; Foundation and construction inspectors
3. Public and private lending institutions should require either a geologic report on the stability of structural sites or a policy of landslide insurance prior to the approval of financing in areas subject to landsliding.[1]	FHA, DVA, Private lending institutions
F. EMERGENCY ACTION FUNCTIONS (Rarely applicable)	
G. OVERALL COGNIZANCE AND COORDINATION FUNCTIONS	
The status of landslide hazards in California should be determined and reported upon annually by the appropriate State agency or agencies. Landsliding should be included among the geologic hazards to be considered by the successor body to the GEC and JCSS after June 30, 1974 (Recommendation 26 in GEC, 1972, p. 55).[1]	CDMG*, MGB

[1] Essentially a new program
[2] Expansion of 1972 programs

* = Lead or co-lead agency
Bold-face type = Major recommendation of Urban Geology Master Plan

Recommended Programs

IV. FLOODING

The natural causes and processes of flooding lie mainly in the fields of weather science and hydrologic engineering, largely outside the field of strictly geotechnical science, so are treated only generally in the Urban Geology Master Plan. On the other hand, the methods and responsibilities for reducing life and property losses from flooding are similar in many respects to those for several of the other geologic problems included in this study. The magnitude of expectable flooding losses—$6.5 billion by 2000, fourth among the 10 geologic problems considered in this study—justifies further consideration of all feasible loss-reduction actions.

It is recommended that the Department of Water Resources, in coordination with other State, federal, and local agencies, make an assessment of existing flood damage prevention measures, future needs, and programs to meet the needs. Loss-reduction measures which should be considered include:

- Weather research.
- Hydrologic research.
- Flood zone mapping, at various scales.
- Consistent, complete socio-economic data on flood damage.
- Improved design and construction practice for dams, levees, weirs.
- Improved public information, especially about "drainage problems" (local flooding)
- Flood information clearinghouse, statewide.
- Flood-zone ordinances.
- Flood insurance policy and practice.
- Flood-zone construction lending policies and practices.
- Traditional government policies regarding: emergency fund grants, low-cost recovery loans, tax-forgiveness.
- Standards for feasibility studies prior to authorizing flood-control works (e.g. Framework Study Program).
- Indemnification of flood-zone landowners for reduced land-use capability under more restrictive flood-zone regulations.
- Model language to permit inclusion of flood and drainage problems in general plan, safety elements.
- Measures for enforcing flood zone regulations.
- Standards for "floodproof" construction.
- Guidance for local governments to include flooding and drainage problems in their emergency-response planning.
- Provide for ongoing top-level cognizance, coordination of all measures to reduce losses from flooding.
- Public purchase of flood-prone areas for open space and park land in lieu of construction of flood-control works.

V. EROSION ACTIVITY

Recommended Programs	Recommended Agencies
A. DATA DEVELOPMENT FUNCTIONS	
1. Develop research data on erosion.	
a. Research into technical, scientific processes that cause or affect erosion.	
i. The geologic processes that contribute to erosion are relatively well known and do not warrant high-priority research programs. The erosion and sedimentation problems that accompany flooding, landsliding, and volcanic events should be considered during research in those problems.[3]	Appropriate research agencies
ii. Coastal erosion processes are more specialized and require research into basic processes and factors aimed at prevention and control measures, especially in urban areas.[2]	USGS, USCE•, DNOD, CDMG, Universities
iii. The many factors that contribute to erosion problems of surficial geologic units under various conditions, and their relationships, should be identified and listed for systematic application in studies of erosion problems in California, including local government planning projects.[3]	SCS
b. Extend inventory of knowledge about erosion in California, including coastal erosion. Those types of soils and rock units that are especially susceptible to erosion under natural, undisturbed conditions should be mapped and described throughout California, and especially in areas subject to coastal erosion.	SCS•, USCE•

[1] Essentially a new program
[2] Expansion of 1972 programs
[3] Continue program at 1972 level

• = Lead or co-lead agency
Bold-face type = Major recommendation of Urban Geology Master Plan

Recommended Programs	Recommended Agencies
i. Statewide compilation scale (1:250,000–1:1,000,000).[1]	SCS*, USCE*
ii. County/regional scale (1:62,500–1:125,000).[2]	SCS*, USCE*
iii. Detail or quadrangle scale, especially in coastal erosion areas (1:12,000–1:24,000).[2]	SCS*, USCE*
iv. Project-scale mapping, for land-use permit decisions or construction purposes (1:1200–1:12,000).[2]	Consultants for local governments, Developers
c. Develop socio-economic analysis information.	
i. Develop a standard procedure for collecting erosion-loss figures separate from landslide and flooding-loss figures.[1]	SCS
ii. Collect and compile reliable figures (per A-c-i) on losses due to erosion, and the costs of erosion-preventive and remedial measures, for standard reporting areas and periods.[1]	Local government
d. Research into engineering response to erosion. Standard engineering practice and state of the art, in predicting erosion danger and in devising measures to control it, is effective and should be applied without exception, considering erosion caused by construction projects, and ongoing erosion in adjacent areas that threatens those projects.[3]	Universities, AEG, ASCE
2. Information-dissemination program.	
a. General public information. Produce an updated, interpretive general purpose primer discussing California's erosion problems as geological hazards. Emphasize the geotechnical nature of the problem, related factors, what can and should be done to reduce losses, and what all this means to the urban area in general, and the homeowner in particular.[2]	SCS*, USDA
b. Information clearinghouse, data-bank program. Improve present information-handling capability and procedures and establish regular ongoing function as clearinghouse for all information about erosion in California.[2]	SCS
B. PLANNING FUNCTIONS	
1. Land-use planning.	
a. Erosion-prone conditions of the undisturbed surface are rarely threatening enough to influence land-use planning. However, procedures for dealing with those rare situations in which an important erosion threat is inherent in local surficial conditions should be made known to all planners.[2]	SCS*, CIR, OPR, AIP, LCC, CSAC, AEG
b. Procedures should be developed for dealing with land-use implications of erosion of coastal cliffs and near-shore features, and model language provided to all planning agencies.[2]	OPR, CIR*, USCE, AIP, LCC, CSAC, USGS, CDMG, AEG
2. Recovery planning.	
a. Include erosion-damage loss among the geologic losses covered by recommended broad-coverage natural disaster insurance program.[1]	FIA*, DI*, FHA, DVA, Insurance industry
C. ENGINEERING FUNCTIONS	
1. Make erosion prevention and control considerations part of design and construction practice for drainage works (e.g., storm drains, culverts, bypass or overflow channels).[2]	Public works agencies, all levels of government, Contractors
2. Plan, design, and build coastal erosion control structures (e.g., seawalls,	USCE*, DNOD

[1] Essentially a new program
[2] Expansion of 1972 programs
[3] Continue program at 1972 level

* = Lead or co-lead agency
Bold-face type = Major recommendation of Urban Geology Master Plan

Recommended Programs	Recommended Agencies
groins, revetments) that have been determined to be necessary and feasible.[3]	
D. ENABLING FUNCTIONS	
1. Adopt improved land-use plans, grading ordinances, and building codes that incorporate model provisions for dealing with erosion, and provide sufficient funds to carry out work programs.[2]	City councils, Boards of Supervisors
2. Improve guidelines and models for proper consideration of erosion in grading ordinances and building codes; include model procedures for enforcing the ordinances and codes; include considerations of potential erosion damage in environmental impact procedures.[2]	CIR*, OPR, SCS, ASCE, AEG
E. ENFORCEMENT FUNCTIONS	
Carry out inspection procedures relative to erosion problems, to enforce compliance with building codes and grading ordinances.[3]	City and county building and grading department inspectors
F. EMERGENCY-RESPONSE FUNCTIONS (Not applicable)	
G. OVERALL COGNIZANCE AND COORDINATION	
The status of erosion problems in California should be determined and reported upon annually by the appropriate State agency or agencies. Erosion activity should be included among the geologic hazards to be considered by the successor body to the GEC and JCSS after June 30, 1974 (Recommendation 26 in GEC, 1972, p. 55).	(body to be established)

VI. EXPANSIVE SOILS

The Subdivision Map Act requires that soils reports be made before subdivisions are approved unless the requirement is waived by local government. Soils reports include detection of expansive soils so that proper action can be taken. The measures that practically eliminate danger of structural damages in expansive soils are relatively inexpensive, well known, and reliable. As long as local officials are adequately funded and diligent in requiring that the soils report information be used properly, losses due to expansive soils can be minimized.

Detailed recommendations of programs to reduce losses from expansive soils are unnecessary in the Urban Geology Master Plan.

VII. FAULT DISPLACEMENT

The recommendations of the Governor's Earthquake Council to reduce losses from seismic events (GEC, 1972) also cover losses from fault displacement.

Likewise, the work of the Joint Committee on Seismic Safety of the California Legislature to generate legislative and other actions to reduce losses from seismic events will also cover losses from fault displacement.

In 1972, Chapter 7.5, the Alquist-Priolo Geologic Hazard Zones Act, proposed by the JCSS, was added to Division 2 of the Public Resources Code. Its purpose is to establish policies and criteria to assist cities, counties, and state agencies in providing for public safety in hazardous fault zones. In 1973, special studies zones are being delineated to encompass potentially hazardous faults in California by the State Geologist. By December 31, 1973,

[2] Expansion of 1972 programs
[3] Continue program at 1972 level
* = Lead or co-lead agency

Bold-face type = Major recommendation of Urban Geology Master Plan

Recommended Programs	Recommended Agencies
the State Mining and Geology Board will have developed policies and criteria to be used in approving all proposed new real estate developments or structures for human occupancy to be placed in the designated special studies zones. Rather than duplicate these efforts, the Urban Geology Master Plan refers to the publications of the GEC, JCSS, and the Alquist-Priolo Act project and endorses their recommendations and procedures.	

VIII. VOLCANIC HAZARDS

A. DATA DEVELOPMENT FUNCTIONS

Recommended Programs	Recommended Agencies
1. Research programs to develop data on volcanic hazard phenomena.	
a. **Field and laboratory research in geotechnical processes involved in volcanism and the forms of volcanic phenomena that occur in California. Apply results of volcanic research conducted outside California in reducing potential volcanic losses in the state. Develop procedures and instruments necessary for a volcanic warning system.**[2]	USGS*, Universities, CDMG
b. Update and refine maps and text descriptions of potential volcanic hazard areas in California. Develop data on probable recurrence and projected damage levels, wherever damage is possible.[3]	CDMG, USGS, Universities, DWR, National Weather Service
i. Statewide scale: update as feasible (1:250,000–1:1,000,000)[1]	CDMG
ii. County/regional scale program (1:62,500–1:125,000)[1]	CDMG, USGS*
iii. Detail or quadrangle scale program (1:12,000–1:24,000)[1]	CDMG*, USGS, Universities, All agencies
c. Gather socio-economic information and analyses. Develop standard procedure for gathering consistent and meaningful data on volcanic hazard losses. Whenever volcanic events occur, gather and analyze the necessary socio-economic data.[1]	Local government, All agencies, Universities
d. Whenever volcanic eruptions occur in California or nearby states, study site and surrounding region to understand the processes involved and to improve capability for predicting that type of event.[1]	CDMG, USGS*, Universities
2. Information dissemination programs.	
Prepare and distribute basic educational materials about volcanic hazards in general, emphasizing local and regional applications and what local residents should know and do about them.[2]	CDMG*, USGS
Establish a clearinghouse and data-bank program for information on volcanic hazards.[1]	CDMG*, USGS

B. PLANNING PROGRAMS

Recommended Programs	Recommended Agencies
1. Land-use planning. Volcanic hazards in California occur primarily in rural areas where land-custody agencies and utilities should consider the threat in their land-use plans.[1]	BLM, USFS, USBR, SCS, DWR, SLD
2. Long-range recovery planning. Extend natural disaster insurance program to cover damage from volcanic phenomena.[2]	DI*, FAIR, FIA*, Insurance industry

[1] Essentially a new program
[2] Expansion of 1972 programs
* = Lead or co-lead agency

Bold-face type = Major recommendation of Urban Geology Master Plan

Recommended Programs	Recommended Agencies
C. ENGINEERING FUNCTIONS	
In designing dams down-drainage from possible volcanic mudflows or within potential ash fall region, consider possible ways to protect vulnerable parts (intakes, generators, valves) from potential volcanic debris.[1]	Dam building agencies: DWR, USCE, USBR, USFS, SCS, Power companies: PG & E, DWP, MWD, SCE
D. ENABLING FUNCTIONS	
Produce handbook for planners and administrators to make them fully aware of volcanic hazards and their implications for land-use planning, and how to apply available geotechnical and other information on the subject.[1]	CDMG, USGS*
E. ENFORCEMENT FUNCTIONS (Not applicable)	
F. EMERGENCY-ACTION FUNCTIONS	
Include volcanic hazards among the natural dangers considered by all emergency-action plans in areas that are potentially vulnerable to this threat.[1]	OEP, OES*, DCPA, USGS, CDMG, Cities, Counties, Utilities, Law enforcement (All agencies concerned with disaster planning)
G. OVERALL COGNIZANCE AND COORDINATION	
The status of volcanic hazards in California should be determined and reported upon annually by the appropriate State agency or agencies. Volcanic hazards should be included among the geologic hazards to be considered by the successor body to the GEC and JCSS after June 30, 1974 (Recommendation 26 in GEC, 1972, p. 55).[1]	USGS, CDMG*

IX. TSUNAMI HAZARDS

Recommended Programs	Recommended Agencies
A. DATA DEVELOPMENT FUNCTIONS	
1. Research programs to develop data on tsunamis.	
a. Research into geologic and seismic processes and bathymetric and coastal configurations that cause or affect seismic sea waves.	
i. Investigate the geologic and seismic processes involved in the generation and transmission of seismic sea waves. Aim is to develop capability to reduce damage from them, and to improve capability to predict them.[3]	NOAA*, USGS, ONR, Universities
ii. Survey and analyze the coastal shelf of California, to define and understand the relationship of bathymetric and coastal configurations to tsunami effects on the coastline. Analyze the relationship of local detail of bottom configuration to expectable local tsunami damage.[2]	USCE, NOAA*, USGS, ONR, DNOD, Universities
iii. Conduct field and laboratory investigations of seiche processes, and other wave-resonance phenomena to evaluate potential for seiche damage at vulnerable points of California's coast and interior lakes and reservoirs.[1]	USCE, NOAA*, USGS, ONR, USBR, DWR, Universities
iv. Establish a system of reliable tide gages specifically to detect and measure tsunami and seiche waves. Instruments must measure minor as well as major events and remain operable in calamitous events.[2]	NOAA*, ONR, USCE, Universities

[1] Essentially a new program
[2] Expansion of 1972 programs
* = Lead or co-lead agency

Bold-face type = Major recommendation of Urban Geology Master Plan

Recommended Programs	Recommended Agencies
v. Correlate tsunami-generation research with fault-displacement and seismic research in the Channel Islands area. Develop means for predicting, or at least detecting swiftly, the kinds of fault movement there that could repeat the monstrous sea waves that reportedly overran the Channel Coast in 1812.[1]	NOAA*, Universities, USGS, CDMG
b. Distribution of seismic sea wave problems.	
i. Gather complete historic record of tsunamis and seiches that have been detected in California. Analyze historic and newly occurring seiches to determine probable recurrence rates of events of varying severity at vulnerable locations.[2]	NOAA*, USGS, Universities, DNOD, DWR
ii. Prepare tsunami/seiche hazard map of California, using historic data and bottom configuration analysis data.	CDMG
Compilation scale program (1 : 250,000–1 : 1,000,000) Update, improve detail on CDMG map (1 : 1,000,000, July 1972; figure 6, this report).[3]	NOAA*, USGS, USCE, DNOD, CDMG
County/regional scale program (1 : 62,500–1 : 125,000) Emphasize threats for which local government should prepare.[2]	NOAA, USGS*, USCE, CDMG, DWR, DNOD, County consultants
Detail or quadrangle scale program (1 : 12,000–1 : 24,000) Delineate in detail conditions of threat at those localities facing appreciable threat.[1]	NOAA, DWR, Local government* (consultants)
Project-scale mapping, for land-use permit decisions or construction purposes (1″ = 100′ to 1″ = 1,000′). Delineate past and possible future runup areas, and depths. Indicate topographic factors that could divert waves and surges. Relate to expectable variations in tide and sea-state conditions.[1]	Local government (consultants)
c. Develop socio-economic information and analyses.	
i. Develop standard procedure, for local government use, for gathering complete and consistent socio-economic data on the costs of seismic sea waves, including costs of damage and of preventive or remedial measures.[1]	Universities, NOAA, USGS, CIR*, DNOD, USCE
ii. Produce reliable statistical data on seismic sea-wave costs (per procedure 1-c-i above) both for past events, by analyzing historical data, and for each new event that occurs.[1]	Local government, NOAA*, USGS, CDMG, DNOD, USCE
d. Research into engineering response to tsunamis.	
i. Investigate behavior of waterfront structures, such as channels, breakwaters and seawalls, wharves, and mooring basins, in response to tsunami experience in California and elsewhere. Develop standards for "tsunami-proofing" typical waterfront structures.[1]	AIA, USCE*, ICBO, DNOD, ASCE, ONR, USCG
ii. Investigate means of preventing or controlling runup and other expectable sea-wave and seiche effects, or at least reducing damage, by building structures (e.g., seawalls, groins).[2]	USCE*, DNOD, DWR
e. Event-study projects.	
i. Whenever a tsunami causes damage to California, conduct detailed study of the nature of the wave itself, and its effects and damage to protective structures. Analyze the performance of utilitarian structures for their resistance to that event, and analyze wave-control structures for their effectiveness in reducing damage from that event.[2]	NOAA, USCE*, ASCE, Universities, ONR, USCG, DNOD, AEG

[1] Essentially a new program
[2] Expansion of 1972 programs
[3] Continue program at 1972 level

* = Lead or co-lead agency
Bold-face type = Major recommendation of Urban Geology Master Plan

Recommended Programs	Recommended Agencies
ii. After event, analyze effectiveness of the event-study procedures, instrumentation, and other detection and response measures.[2]	All event-study agencies
2. Information-dissemination programs	
a. Produce basic public information on tsunami processes and their importance for California. Aim for schools, government officials, and broad public audience. Include: What to expect from tsunamis and how to survive them.[2]	CDMG*, USGS, NOAA, USCG, DNOD
b. Devise clearinghouse and data-bank program for all information on seismic sea waves.[2]	**NOAA* All tsunami information-producing agencies. All tsunami information-using agencies.**
B. PLANNING FUNCTIONS	
1. Land-use planning.	
a. Produce interpretive general-use manual to apprise planners of sea wave hazards in general, and of vulnerable localities in particular. Describe the potential dangers and possible land-use planning actions to reduce losses, including standards for exclusion zones, permissible activities, and "tsunami-proof" construction. List the available maps, materials, and services, and describe their applications.[1]	NOAA, USGS, AIP, CIR*, DNOD, CDMG (information)
b. Adopt standards and procedures for the land-use planning process that require adequate consideration of tsunami and seiche hazards. Revise general plans as necessary to incorporate effective model of seismic sea wave hazard element (within seismic safety element), employing current state of the art.[1]	City and county planning departments, Regional government, Land-custody agencies: SLD, DPR, BLM
2. Recovery planning	
Extend natural disaster insurance program to cover seismic sea wave damage.[1]	DI*, FAIR, FIA*, Insurance industry
C. ENGINEERING FUNCTIONS	
1. If and when feasibility studies prove them to be desirable, build local sea-wave control structures (sea-walls, breakwaters, diversion levees) to stop or divert water surges, and reduce casualties and damage to onshore facilities and structures, and shipping.[2]	USCE*, DNOD, Harbor and port districts
2. Apply "tsunami-proof" design and construction principles to structures that need to be in zones threatened by sea waves so they can be removed or made impervious to tsunami damage on short notice.[1]	USCE*, DNOD, Harbor and port districts, Shipping and sea-front industries
D. ENABLING FUNCTIONS	
1. Political and administrative actions	
a. Provide authority and policy guidance. Adopt tsunami and seiche provisions in local government land-use plans (general plan) and adopt zoning and other ordinances and regulations necessary for implementation.[3]	City councils, Boards of Supervisors, Land-custody agencies, Utility agencies
b. Provide resources. Approve funding and manpower to carry out inspections, reviews, and other actions required to accomplish the purposes of the plans, codes, ordinances and regulations.[1]	City councils, Boards of Supervisors, Land-custody agencies, Utility agencies
2. Coordinative, information guidelines	
a. Produce guidelines for treating sea-wave danger in the seismic safety element of general plans, including model language.[1]	CIR*, OPR, CDMG (information)

[1] Essentially a new program
[2] Expansion of 1972 programs
[3] Continue program at 1972 level

* = Lead or co-lead agency
Bold-face type = Major recommendation of Urban Geology Master Plan

Recommended Programs	Recommended Agencies
b. Produce model "Sea-wave hazard zone" ordinance, and procedure for enforcing it.[1]	OPR*, CIR, AIP
c. Develop guidelines and interpretive information on the effects of sea-wave hazards on environmental impact decisions.[1]	OPR*, CIR, EPA, OIM
E. ENFORCEMENT FUNCTIONS	
1. Executive and administrative control	
a. Apply appropriate safety principles in approving construction and use permits in areas subject to seismic sea waves.[1]	Local government Planning commissions, City councils, Boards of Supervisors
b. After a realistic deadline, require that specified actions to reduce tsunami losses be effectively taken by local jurisdictions in coastal areas before granting further funds to those jurisdictions for coastal studies, coastal planning and related activities.[1]	Funds-dispensing agencies: HUD*, CIR, NSF, OEP, OES
2. Operational inspection	
a. Inspect construction and other developments in locations subject to seismic sea wave hazards as necessary to assure compliance with safety regulations, and zoning, grading, and building ordinances.[1]	Local government grading, foundation, and construction inspectors, Land-custody agencies, Utility agencies
3. Insurance organizations should require evidence that seismic sea-wave dangers have been properly considered and loss-reduction measures taken before insuring structures in tsunami hazard areas.[2]	Insurance companies, Board of Underwriters
4. Construction and development loans should not be approved for structures in tsunami hazard areas until lending institutions are assured that proper damage avoidance or prevention action will be taken.[1]	FHA*, DVA*, Lending organizations
F. EMERGENCY-RESPONSE FUNCTION	
1. Provide overall guidelines and coordination to help local governments and land-custodial agencies cope with tsunami emergencies. Develop and disseminate guidelines for local governments and land-custody agencies on the use of the federal Seismic Sea Wave Warning System in disaster-readiness procedures. Include guidelines for tsunami preparedness measures.[1]	NOAA, USGS, OEP, OES*, DCPA, AIP, AEG
2. Develop contingency plans	
a. Include consideration of seismic sea wave and seiche hazards in emergency planning procedures of local governments, land-custody agencies, and public utility type agencies; produce elements of emergency response plans that properly prepare to cope with these hazards.[1]	OES*, CIR, OPR, LCC, CSAC, Local government emergency-planning agencies: Police, Fire, Sheriff; Communications media, including private sector
b. Adopt emergency-response plans, and carry out the pre-event preparations called for therein.[2]	City councils, Boards of Supervisors, Land-custody agencies, Utility agencies
3. When tsunamis occur, activate contingency plans.[3]	All agencies

[1] Essentially a new program
[2] Expansion of 1972 programs
[3] Continue program at 1972 level

* = Lead or co-lead agency
Bold-face type = Major recommendation of Urban Geology Master Plan

Recommended Programs	Recommended Agencies
G. OVERALL COGNIZANCE AND COORDINATION FUNCTIONS	
The status of tsunami hazards in California should be determined and reported upon annually by the appropriate State agency or agencies. Tsunamis should be included among the geologic hazards to be considered by the successor body to the GEC and JCSS after June 30, 1974 (Recommendation 26 in GEC, 1972, p. 55).[1]	(body to be established)
X. SUBSIDENCE	
A. DATA FUNCTIONS	
1. Research programs to develop data on subsidence.	
a. Basic research into processes that cause or influence subsidence in California. Develop capacity to predict where and how severe subsidence will be under various types of use. Devise and improve ways to prevent subsidence, ameliorate damage from it, and to detect it in incipient stages.[2]	USGS*, DWR*, Universities, SCS, CDOG*, Oil and gas industry, Geothermal industry
b. Map and describe areas of actual and potential subsidence in California.	USGS*, CDOG*, CDMG, SCS, DWR*
i. Statewide compilation scale (1:250,000–1:1,000,000).[3]	DWR*, CDMG, USGS*
ii. County/regional scale (1:62,500–1:125,000).[2]	CDMG, DWR*, USGS*, CDOG*
iii. Detail or quadrangle scale especially in areas of groundwater withdrawal and potential hydrocompaction (1:12,000–1:24,000).[2]	DWR*, CDOG*, USGS*, SLD
2. Data-dissemination programs.	
a. Produce and disseminate educational information on subsidence for general public use, emphasizing regional and local occurrences.[2]	DWR*, CDMG, USGS, CDOG*, Education agencies, Mass media
b. Establish clearinghouse and data-bank functions for all subsidence data and information of use in California.[2]	DWR*, CDMG, CDOG*, USGS, All data-producing agencies, All data-using agencies
c. Socio-economic analysis research.	
Develop procedures and gather data, in consistent units and format, for evaluating losses due to subsidence, and the costs of loss-reduction measures. One aim is to determine where subsidence is actually damaging, and damage costs.[1]	Universities (economics depts.), CDOG*, DWR*, USGS*, Cities, Counties, Land-custody agencies
d. Research into engineering response to subsidence.	
i. Continue to investigate the response behavior of local surficial materials in subsidence-prone localities to various types of construction, so that structures can be located and designed to avoid damage.[2]	USGS*, DWR*, AEG, ICBO, ASCE, SEAOC
ii. Investigate design and construction standards for foundations (including site preparation) and for structures to be placed in localities subject to subsidence, including public utility and industrial structures.[2]	ICBO*, ASCE, SEAOC
e. Event-study research: Continue to investigate known subsidence situations, with the aim of determining the cost-effectiveness of loss-reduction measures.[2]	DWR*, USGS*, CDOG*, Oil and gas industry, ASCE, AEG, Universities

[1] Essentially a new program
[2] Expansion of 1972 programs
[3] Continue program at 1972 level

* = Lead or co-lead agency
Bold-face type = Major recommendation of Urban Geology Master Plan

Recommended Programs	Recommended Agencies
B. PLANNING FUNCTIONS	
1. Land-use planning. Prepare handbook for planners, interpreting what is known of the process and local detail of subsidence in terms of its impact for land-use planning procedures. The handbook should develop effective procedures, including model language, for incorporating pertinent subsidence hazard information into the land-use planning procedures of local governments and land-custody agencies. It should consider the subsidence threat in relation to use-capability of land, zoning procedures, and conditions to be imposed on development or use; in effect, incorporating subsidence consideration, when appropriate, into the geologic hazards considered in the preparation of safety elements of general plans.[2]	DWR, CDMG, USGS, OPR, CIR*, LCC, CSAC, CDOG, City and county planning departments
In areas undergoing, or subject to, subsidence, prepare or improve the provisions of general plans that deal with subsidence hazards.[2]	City and county planning departments
2. Recovery planning. Develop procedure and practice of including subsidence among the geologic hazards covered under a natural disaster, broad-coverage insurance program.[1]	FIA*, DI*
C. ENGINEERING FUNCTIONS	
Specialized engineering works for dealing with subsidence include injection/repressuring well systems at some oil or geothermal fields; sea-control dikes in some water front lowlands; special pilings, foundation extensions, and anti-submersion provisions for fixed activities in some coastal lowlands; special preparations necessary for developing spreading grounds for groundwater recharge; and canal-level adjustment provisions for some canal-route subsidence localities.	
The agencies responsible for designing, constructing, and monitoring the performance of these structures should continue to review the effectiveness and feasibility of each installation and compare these factors with those for alternate methods of reducing subsidence losses, in terms of local costs and benefits, both short and long-term.[2]	DWR, CDOG, USBR, USCE, Cities, Counties, Special districts
D. ENABLING FUNCTIONS	
Authority and responsibility for oil field and geothermal field-related subsidence are sufficient to deal with the problem, once it is recognized. Groundwater withdrawal subsidence is part of the major problem of groundwater basin management, which requires comprehensive concern for water quality and quantity. Except for water quality control efforts under the Porter-Cologne Act, controls on groundwater removal in California are exercised only by a few local governments without direct State control.	
Hydrocompaction and peat soil subsidence, as essentially surficial problems, are coped with in various degrees by the owners of the local surface rights without direct control by government at any level.	
E. ENFORCEMENT FUCTIONS (Not applicable)	
F. EMERGENCY-RESPONSE FUNCTIONS (Not applicable)	
G. OVERALL COGNIZANCE AND COORDINATION FUNCTIONS	
The status of subsidence problems in California should be determined and reported upon annually by the appropriate State agency or agencies. Subsidence should be included among the geologic hazards to be considered by the successor body to the GEC and JCSS after June 30, 1974 (Recommendation 26 in GEC, 1972, p. 55).[1]	(body to be established)

[1] Essentially a new program
[2] Expansion of 1972 programs

* = Lead or co-lead agency

Section 5

Priorities for Loss–Reduction Programs

Genera

A primary objective of
Plan project is to examine
orities among the possib
and to establish a practica
priority-setting process.
One conclusion derived
several priority-setting s
tors affecting the setting
this section, but specific p
priority listing. This pro
and knowledge of the
organizations to permit
detailed plan.
Priority decisions need
the following factors:

1. Locality (city, county, or
2. Geologic problem for a
wide or statewide project,
3. Particular loss-reduction
problem, or for a chosen locality

The major determinants
allel these three priority fa
locality where loss-reduction
plied first requires evaluation
for loss-reduction work. T
work closely reflects the ma
ens the locality. This is the
ority methodology develope
Geology Master Plan pro
Mines and Geology, 197
ates, in terms of dollar loss
threat of damage inherent
of all the geologic problems
cality, second the number
those problems in that locality
projected population growth

Geologic Haza

During Phase I of this proj
ing the location and degrees
logic problems were compiled
Indicators of the severity were
then digitized on a rectangular
corresponding to 7½-minute
U.S. Geological Survey
Figure 13 shows the compos
all 10 geologic problems.
Each geologic problem wa
ratings in every quadrangle
loss potential for destruction
each degree of severity. Becaus
has not been documented adequ
all of the geologic problems
was required in order to provi

General Statement

A primary objective of the Urban Geology Master Plan project is to examine the problem of setting priorities among the possible loss-reduction programs, and to establish a practical method for improving the priority-setting process.

One conclusion derived from the project was that several priority-setting systems are necessary. The factors affecting the setting of priorities are discussed in this section, but specific projects are not itemized in a priority listing. This project is too limited in authority and knowledge of the work programs of the affected organizations to permit the development of such a detailed plan.

Priority decisions need to be made with respect to the following factors:

1. Locality (city, county, or region).
2. Geologic problem (for a chosen locality or for a county-wide or statewide project).
3. Particular loss-reduction measures (for a chosen geologic problem, or for a chosen locality).

The major determinants for priority decisions parallel these three priority factors. A decision as to the locality where loss-reduction measures should be applied first requires evaluation of the magnitude of need for loss-reduction work. The need for loss-reduction work closely reflects the magnitude of loss that threatens the locality. This is the basic approach of the priority methodology developed in Phase I of the Urban Geology Master Plan project (California Division of Mines and Geology, 1971). That methodology evaluates, in terms of dollar loss, first the magnitude of the threat of damage inherent in the number and severity of all the geologic problems present in any given locality, second the number of people to be exposed to those problems in that locality, and third the timing of projected population growth there.

Geologic Hazard Threat

During Phase I of this project, statewide maps showing the location and degrees of severity of the 10 geologic problems were compiled at a scale of 1:1,000,000. Indicators of the severity zones for each problem were then digitized on a rectangular grid with the cell size corresponding to 7½-minute (latitude and longitude) U.S. Geological Survey topographic quadrangles. Figure 13 shows the composite of severity ratings for all 10 geologic problems.

Each geologic problem was then given numerical ratings in every quadrangle indicative of its dollar loss potential for destruction of life and property for each degree of severity. Because actual loss experience has not been documented adequately in California for all of the geologic problems, a simulative approach was required in order to provide a common basis for comparative evaluation of the threats. A hypothetical urban area, called the "urban unit," of 3,000 population, and $90,000,000 total value (average $30,000 per resident) was devised as a standard typical unit against which to measure the simulated impact of each severity level of each problem.

By simulating placement of the "urban unit" in each severity zone of each geologic problem and calculating the dollar costs of expectable damage, considering loss per event and average recurrence period between events, and assigning a value of $75,000 per life lost (California Division of Mines and Geology, 1971, p. 3–22), a numerical value was assigned that represents the expectable average annual loss to any resident in each severity zone of each problem. This numerical value, expressed as "Geology Points" (GP), then becomes a relative weighting factor for that type of problem for any quadrangle in the indicated severity zone. The sum of the geology points for the different types and degrees of threat present in any specific quadrangle expresses the average dollar loss that the average resident of that quadrangle might expect to suffer per year from all geologic problems.

A representative area of southern California, showing the Geology Point method, appears as figure 21. The rationale and details of the methods used to obtain the Geology Points for all 10 problems are described in Section 7, Appendix A, of this report.

Population Impact

Also during Phase I of this study, the concept was developed that two independent aspects of the population characteristics of each area contribute (along

Geology Points *

Problem	High severity	Medium severity	Low severity
Earthquake shaking	31	27	14
Loss of mineral resources	22	..	..
Landsliding	53	35	1
Flooding	290	96	..
Erosion activity	3	2	1
Expansive soils	3	2	0
Fault displacement	5	0.50	0.06
Volcanic hazards	57	10	3
Tsunami hazards	144	14	1
Subsidence	0.34	0.02	0

NOTE: In this report, where Geology Point values are used in priority calculations and dollar-loss estimations, those GP values larger than 1 are rounded to the nearest whole number, and those smaller than 1 are rounded to one significant figure.

* Geology Point values correspond to anticipated average annual per capita loss in dollars.

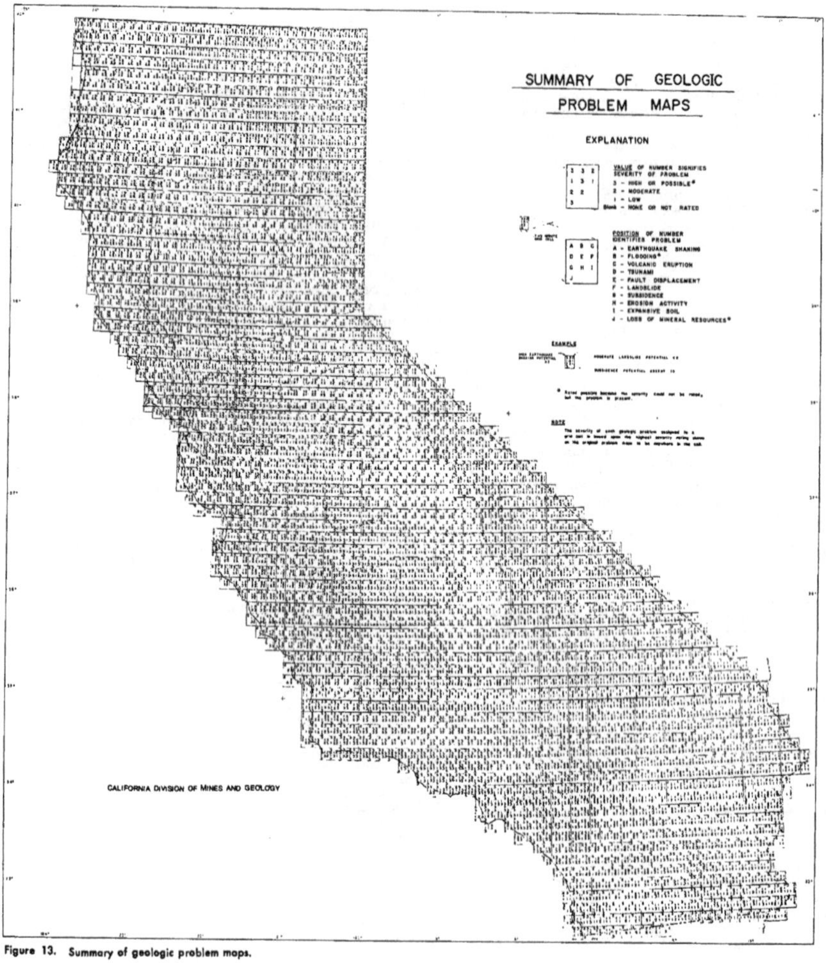

Figure 13. Summary of geologic problem maps.

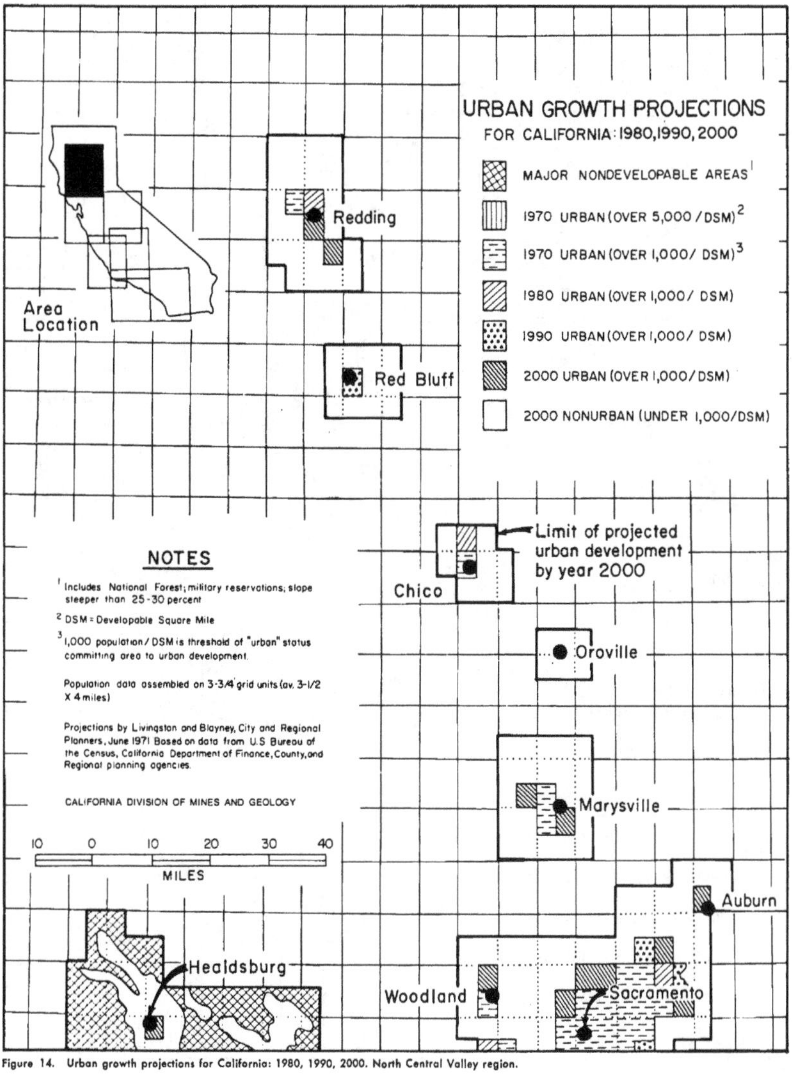
URBAN GROWTH PROJECTIONS
FOR CALIFORNIA: 1980, 1990, 2000
MAJOR NONDEVELOPABLE AREAS[1]
1970 URBAN (OVER 5,000 / DSM)[2]
1970 URBAN (OVER 1,000/ DSM)[3]
1980 URBAN (OVER 1,000/ DSM)
1990 URBAN (OVER 1,000/ DSM)
2000 URBAN (OVER 1,000/DSM)
2000 NONURBAN (UNDER 1,000/DSM)
Area Location
Redding
Red Bluff
Limit of projected urban development by year 2000
Chico
Oroville
Marysville
Auburn
Woodland
Sacramento
Healdsburg
NOTES
[1] Includes National Forest; military reservations; slope steeper than 25-30 percent
[2] DSM = Developable Square Mile
[3] 1,000 population / DSM is threshold of "urban" status committing area to urban development.
Population data assembled on 3-3/4' grid units (av. 3-1/2 X 4 miles)
Projections by Livingston and Blayney, City and Regional Planners, June 1971 Based on data from U.S Bureau of the Census, California Department of Finance, County, and Regional planning agencies.
CALIFORNIA DIVISION OF MINES AND GEOLOGY
10 0 10 20 30 40
MILES

Figure 14. Urban growth projections for California: 1980, 1990, 2000. North Central Valley region.

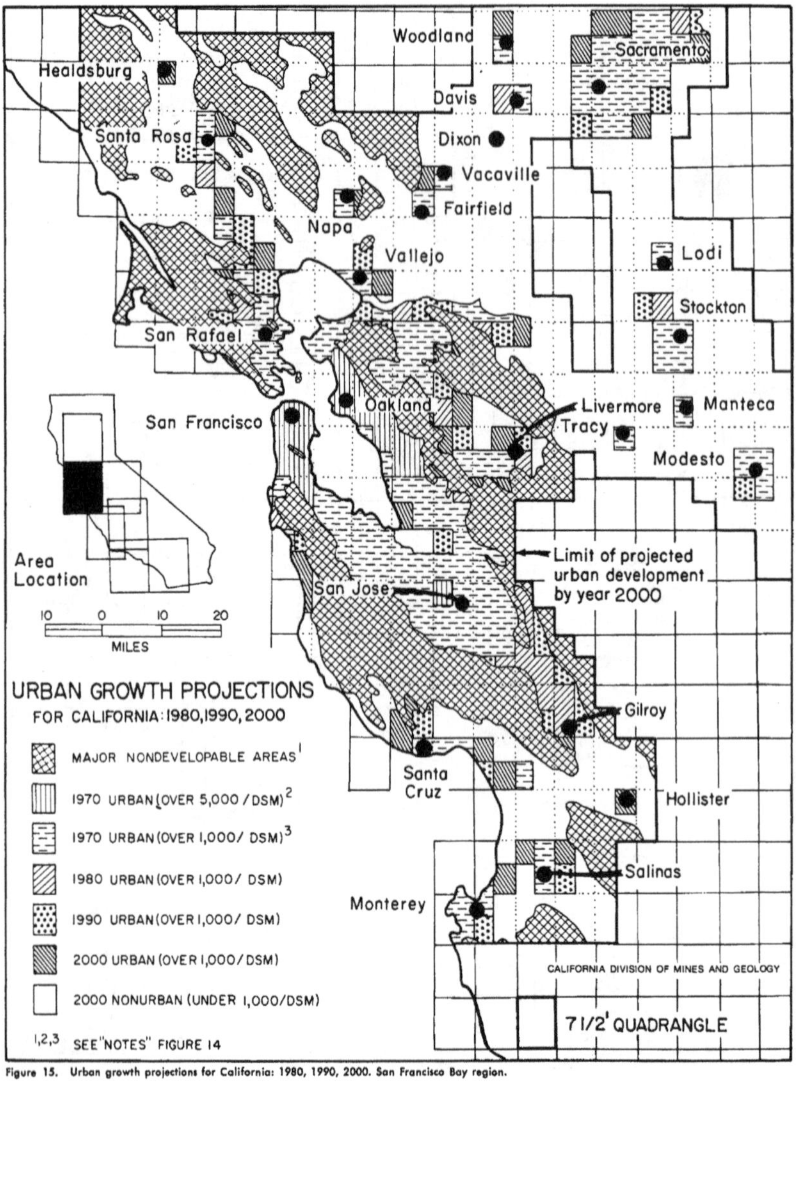

Figure 15. Urban growth projections for California: 1980, 1990, 2000. San Francisco Bay region.

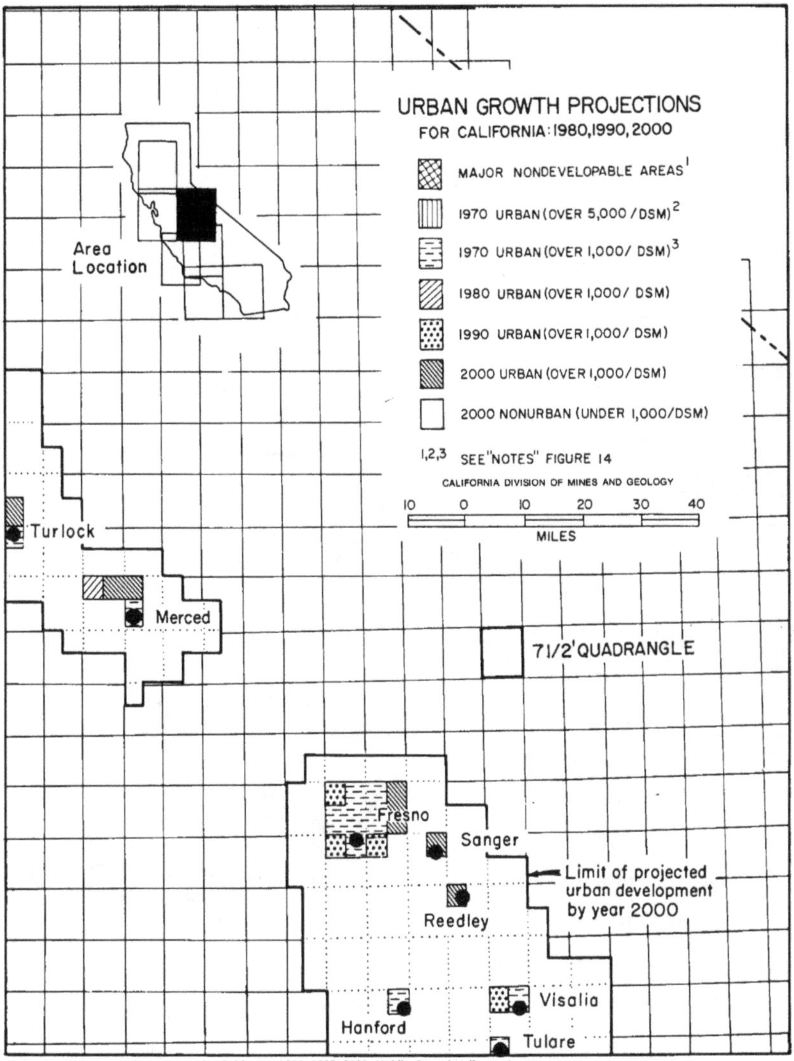

Figure 16. Urban growth projections for California: 1980, 1990, 2000. Middle Central Valley region.

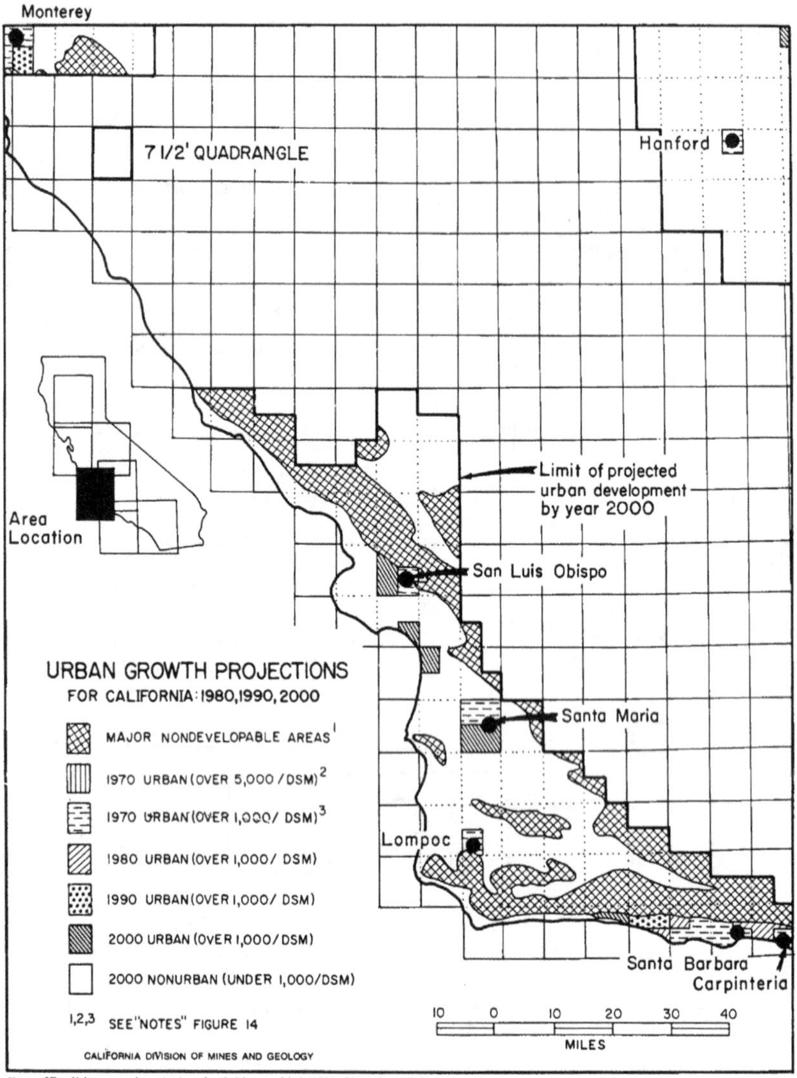

Figure 17. Urban growth projections for California: 1980, 1990, 2000. Central Coastal region.

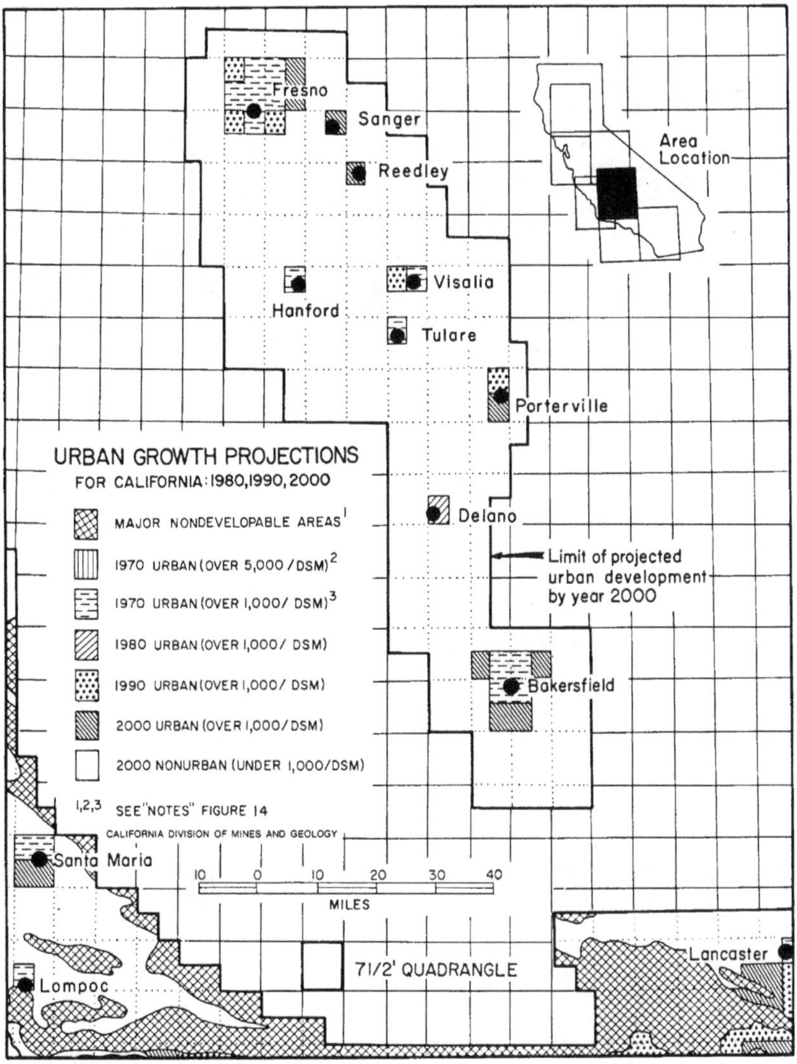

Figure 18. Urban growth projections for California: 1980, 1990, 2000. South Central Valley region.

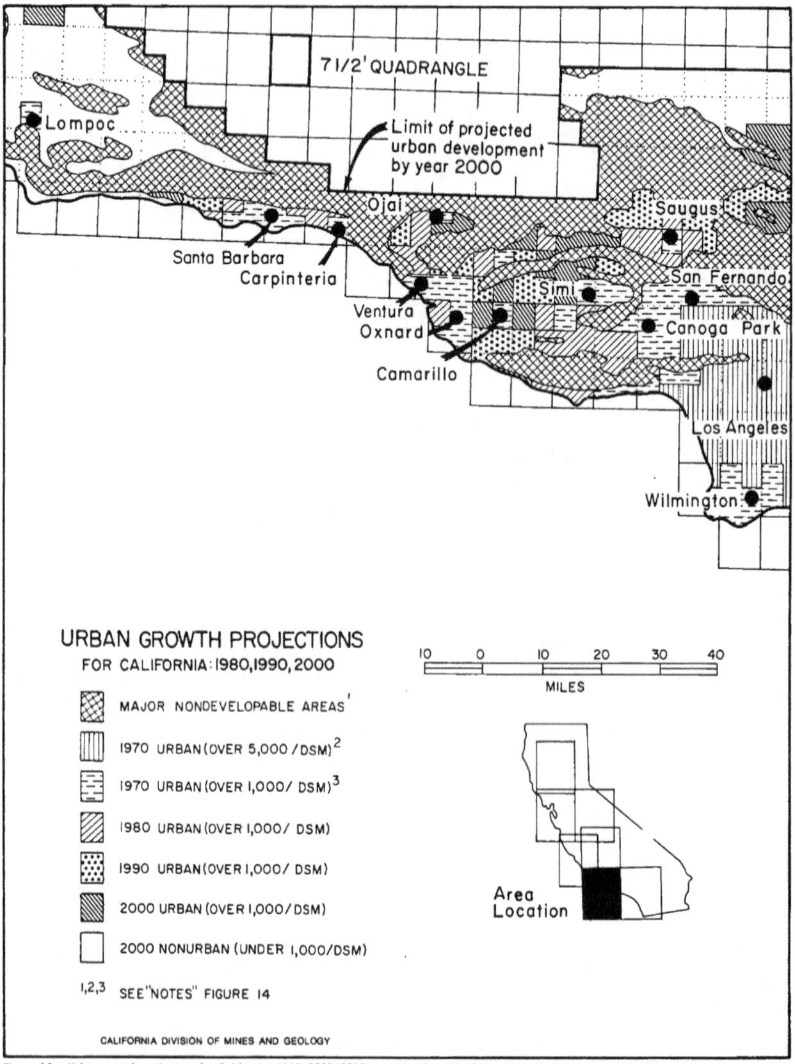

Figure 19. Urban growth projections for California: 1980, 1990, 2000. West Southern California region.

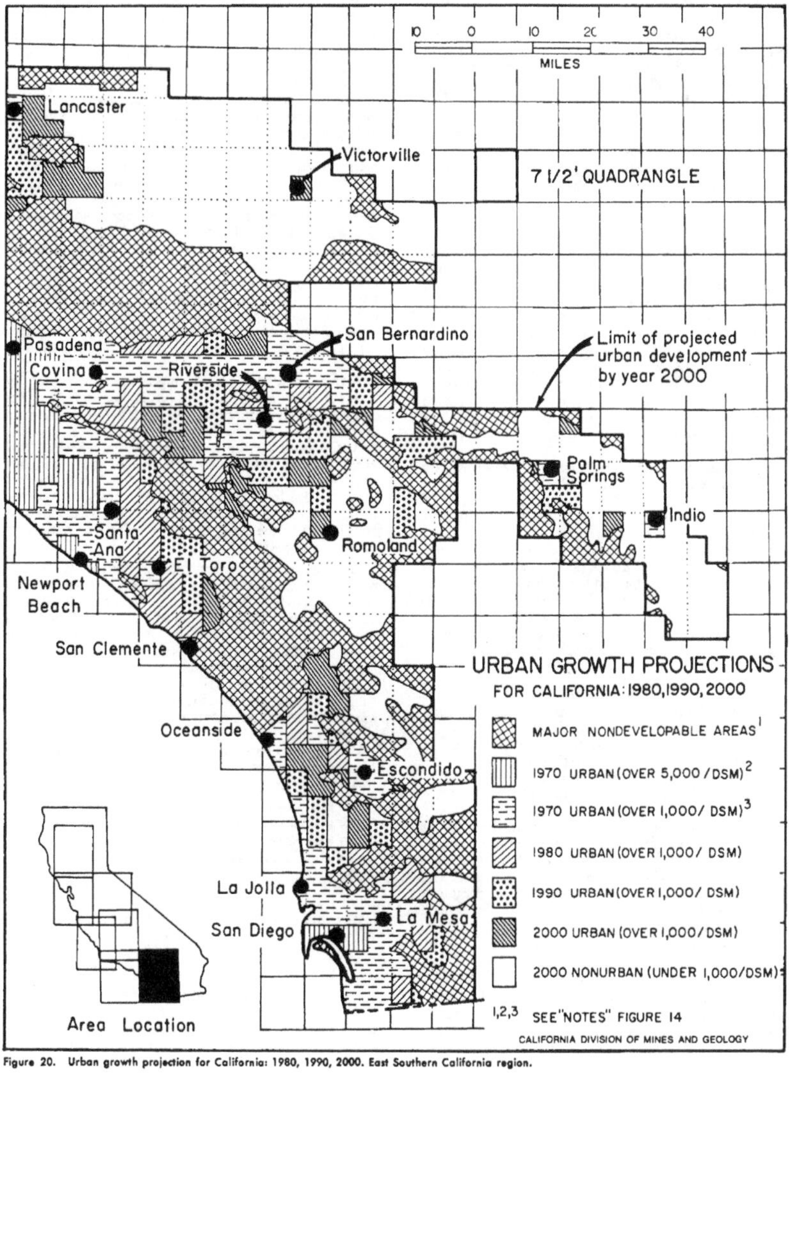

Figure 20. Urban growth projection for California: 1980, 1990, 2000. East Southern California region.

with Geology Points) to the overall priority of that area for geologic study. The projected population levels and densities for the decade years 1970, 1980, 1990, and 2000 were developed for 3¾ minute grid cells (quarters of the 7½ minute quadrangles) and depicted on 1:250,000-scale maps of the urban areas of the State. (Population projections for the urban areas of California are depicted on figures 14–20. Description of the method used in the projection process appears in Section 7, Appendix B, of this report.)

The two fundamental aspects of population considered in this study are (1) the level of population present in any area, and (2) the timing of the buildup in that area to the level that irreversibly commits any area to become "urban" (considered to be 1,000 residents per developable square mile). The population level is expressed in "Person-Years" exposure (PY), defined as the average number of residents projected to be in the area during the three decades considered in this study: 1970–1980; 1980–1990; and 1990–2000. The timing of population growth is expressed as "Immediacy Factor" (IF), a number that expresses the rate of projected growth during the three decades, times a discount factor for present worth at 8 percent per annum, that gives a weight of 4.67 to population growth that takes place in the first decade, and 2.16 and 1.00, respectively, for population growth in the second and third decades.

Areas that had reached full urban development by 1970 (considered to be 5,000 residents per developable square mile) were given an Immediacy Factor of zero (hence zero Priority Points) in Phase I because in these areas it was considered to be already too late to avoid construction in hazardous spots, or to overcome known risks by design and construction measures. In calculating the simulated losses due to the 10 geologic problems, only the impact on residential areas and their supporting structures were considered. No attempt was made to estimate losses to agriculture, forests, unimproved land, or works of man outside of the urban areas.

Priority Points

The Phase I methodology was to multiply the total Geology Points value for a specific quadrangle or locality, times the Person-Years factor for that locality, times the Immediacy Factor for that locality, to yield an overall value called "Priority Points" (PP): GP × PY × IF = PP. The relative ranking of these Priority Point values, computed for every locality, then would indicate the relative priority among quadrangles or localities in California to receive geotechnical investigation. These factors were digitized, by 7½-minute quadrangle grid cells for geologic factors and 3¾-minute grid cells for population factors; and computer programs were devised to record the many values and to combine them rapidly in various configurations to indicate precise numerical priority values.

Revised Values for Priority Point Factors

The numerical values derived in Phase I for Geology Points (Section 7, Appendix A) were revised following further analysis of Phase I rationale, and applying improved loss figures based on actual experience in selected quadrangles studied during Phase II. A major factor of the revision was to increase the life-loss factor from $75,000 per death to $360,000 per death, based on a sampling of court awards in indemnity suits for death and permanent injury, plus hospital costs for associated expectable injuries.

Another major revision was to devise a separate factor for catastrophic losses—an arbitrary "Disaster Factor" that reflects the potential of the more destructive geologic hazards events of possibly disastrous problems such as earthquakes and volcanic eruptions, to escalate into regional catastrophes with far-reaching secondary loss effects, including social and political impact. If life-loss potential is 1 to 10 deaths per single event, a Disaster Factor of 1.1 was assigned (e.g., landslides and fault displacements of high severity); if 11 to 100 lives could be lost, a factor of 1.5 was used (volcanic hazards and earthquakes of low severity); if 101 to 1,000 lives could be lost, the factor was 2 (volcanic eruptions and earthquakes of medium severity); for events that could kill more thas 1,000, the disaster factor was 3 (volcanic eruptions and earthquakes of high severity).

A third major revision during Phase II of this study was the recognition that the dollar loss due to direct physical damage caused by any geologic problem event is matched by an approximately equal dollar loss due to socio-economic, or secondary consequences of that event, such as lost employment, loss of job productivity, lost purchasing power, and other out-of-locality impacts; also legal costs, delays, psychological trauma, losses due to industrial, utility, and infrastructure disruption, and otherwise decreased efficiency before recovery is complete.

A fourth revision was the assignment of an Immediacy Factor value of 1 to all areas that were already urban by 1970, replacing the Phase I value of zero. This gives those considerable areas, such as downtown San Francisco and Los Angeles, Priority Point values indicative of their potential geologic problems, instead of zero. These revised values better indicate the need for certain geologic and seismologic investigations in those places to assist in guiding further development or redevelopment, regardless of their present urban nature.

Combining Phase I methodology and Phase II modifications of values, the Urban Geology Master Plan's final priority factors are:

GP = Geology Points for all problems in that locality
DF = Disaster Factor for those problems in that locality
PY = Person-Years exposure for that locality
IF = Immediacy Factor for that locality

These factors multiplied give the overall Priority Points value, indicating priority to receive geologic loss-reduction work, for any quadrangle or other locality:

GP × DF × PY × IF = PP

Application of Priority Points

As a demonstration and test of the application of the Priority Point rationale and values produced in Phases I and II of this project, numerical values were computed for quadrangles in the state's two main urban areas: the San Francisco Bay area in northern California, and the Los Angeles-San Diego area in southern California. Only the threats of the five geologic problems within the main capabilities of the Division of Mines and Geology were considered in computing these Priority Points, namely, earthquake shaking, loss of mineral deposits, landsliding, fault displacement, and volcanic hazards. The updated Geology Point values, which include all modifications resulting from Phase II studies, were multiplied by the appropriate Disaster Factors (see below), Person-Years exposure, and Immediacy Factor.

	Disaster Factor		
	High	Moderate	Low
Earthquake shaking	3	2	1.5
Loss of mineral deposits	1	1	1
Landslides	1.1	1	1
Fault displacement	1.1	1	1
Volcanic hazards	3	2	1.5

The resulting lists of 3¾ minute quadrangles indicate priorities for loss-reduction work, considering only the numerical factors used for this method.

Southern California

Priority number	Quadrangle	County	Priority points
1	Laguna Beach NE ¼	Orange	50 500
2	Orange SE ¼	Orange	48,400
3	Orange NE ¼	Orange	45,200
4	Newhall SW ¼	Los Angeles	42,700
5	Tustin SW ¼	Orange	37,400
6	Orange SW ¼	Orange	36,750
7	Newhall SE ¼	Los Angeles	36,500
8	Tustin NE ¼	Orange	36,200
9	Laguna Beach NW ¼	Orange	34,950
10	Yorba Linda NW ¼	Los Angeles and Orange	34,700

Northern California

Priority number	Quadrangle	County	Priority points
1	Morgan Hill SE ¼	Santa Clara	22,650
2	Niles SW ¼	Alameda	21,300
3	Palo Alto NW ¼	San Mateo	20,100
4	Palo Alto NE ¼	San Mateo and Santa Clara	19,600
5	San Mateo SW ¼	San Mateo	17,600
6	Morgan Hill SW ¼	Santa Clara	17,000
7	Calaveras Reservoir SW ¼	Santa Clara	16,300
8	Benicia NW ¼	Contra Costa and Solano	16 100
9	San Jose East SW ¼	Santa Clara	14,200
10	Santa Teresa Hills NE ¼	Santa Clara	13,900

Figure 21 illustrates the Geology Points (revised values) and Disaster Factors for a representative segment of the Los Angeles area distributed according to Phase I geologic problems-severity zone maps. Figure 22 illustrates Priority Points for the same area, combining Geology Points, Disaster Factor, Person-Years, and Immediacy Factor values. From figure 22 it is seen that the Priority Point rankings are far more sensitive to variations in the population factors than they are to variations in the Geology Points.

Comparison computations were made for two test areas, one in northern and one in southern California. These comparisons showed that if the Phase I Geology Points were used instead of the revised values obtained in the Phase II study (the Phase I values average about 50 to 100 percent change in values both higher and lower than those obtained in the Phase II study), and all 10 geologic problems were included, instead of just the five of Division of Mines and Geology's prime interest, while the population factors were left unchanged, about two-thirds of the quadrangles fell in the "top ten" lists produced using both methods. Another computation comparing the same areas but using only the population factors (IF $\times$ PY) and ignoring Geology Points and the Disaster Factor altogether produced "top ten" lists with 85 percent overlap, ranked in approximately the same priority order. Both these comparisons indicate that the Priority Points method of selecting priorities gives far more emphasis to the population factors, and mainly to the rate of population buildup in a locality (IF), than to the number and severity of geologic problems that are present.

Needed Refinements of Priority Points

The Priority Point methodology developed during Phases I and II of this project can be further refined by updating and improving the geotechnical detail of the input maps that show what problems are present, and their severity, in each locality. The maps also could be improved by resolving the ambiguity present in many localities, whether "no problem is present" or "we don't know whether a problem is present or not." Another refinement would be to indicate the places where loss-reduction measures have already been taken. In considering the Priority Point method as a guideline for decisions as to where to conduct actual loss-reduction projects, it is clear that some loss-reduction actions may be best done miles away from the site of damage; for instance, distant dams prevent local floods. Although the Priority Points method gives reliable guidance to localities where problems are most severe and threaten the most people, other factors still are needed to determine priorities as to which of several threatening problems should first receive organized statewide attention, or which among several feasible loss-reduction measures should be applied first at a threatened locality.

Priority Considerations by Geologic Problem

Top political and administrative decision makers face the relatively long-range question, "Which among the several geologic problems that face California should receive the most emphasis?" Having a relatively fixed sum to spend on all geologic problems,

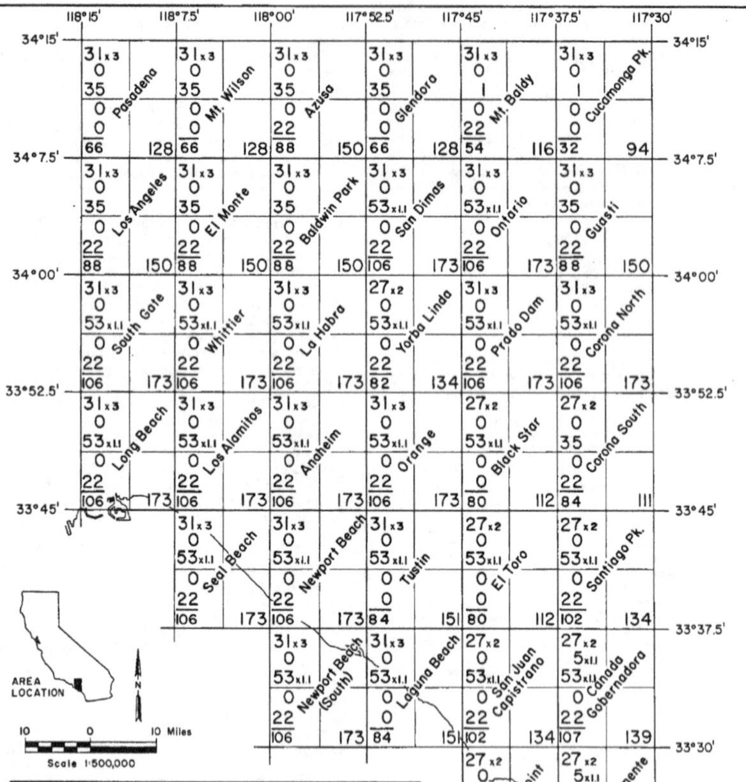

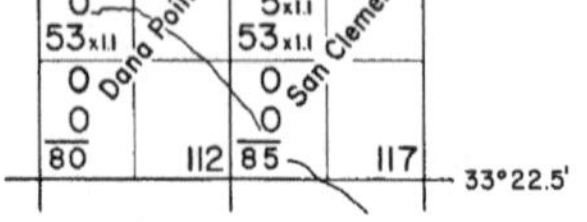

GEOLOGY POINTS (GP) AND DISASTER FACTORS (DF)										
Severity Zone	Earthquake Shaking		Fault Displacement		Landsliding		Volcanic Hazards		Loss of Mineral Deposits	
	GP	DF	GP	DF	GP	DF	GP	DF	GP	DF
High	31	3	5	1.1	53	1.1	57	3	22	—
Moderate	27	2	1	—	35	—	10	2	none	—
Low	14	1.5	0	—	1	—	3	1.5	none	—
Nil	none	—	0	—	0	—	0	—	0	—

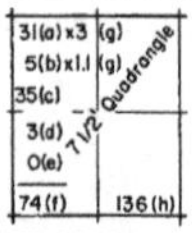

QUADRANGLE EXAMPLE

GEOLOGY POINT VALUES (ROUNDED)

(a) For earthquake shaking.
(b) For fault displacement.
(c) For landsliding.
(d) For volcanic hazards.
(e) For loss of mineral deposits.
(f) Total geology points for 7 1/2' quadrangle

(g) DISASTER FACTORS

Disaster Factor	Potential Life-Loss Per Event
3	more than 1,000
2	101–1,000
1.5	11–100
1.1	1–10

(h) Sum of Geology Points multiplied by appropriate Disaster Factors

GEOLOGY POINTS
AND DISASTER FACTORS
(SAMPLE AREA, SELECTED TO SHOW METHODOLOGY)

CALIFORNIA DIVISION OF MINES AND GEOLOGY

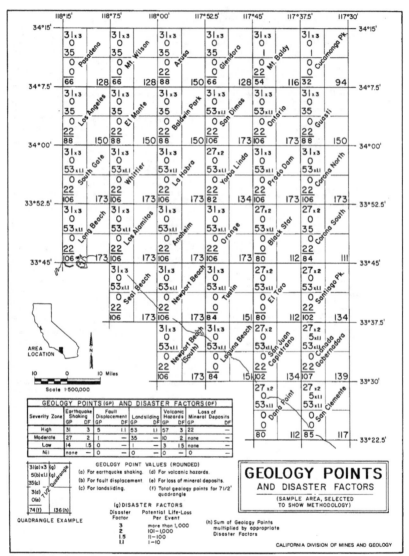

Figure 21. Geology Points and Disaster Factors. Sample area selected to show methodology.

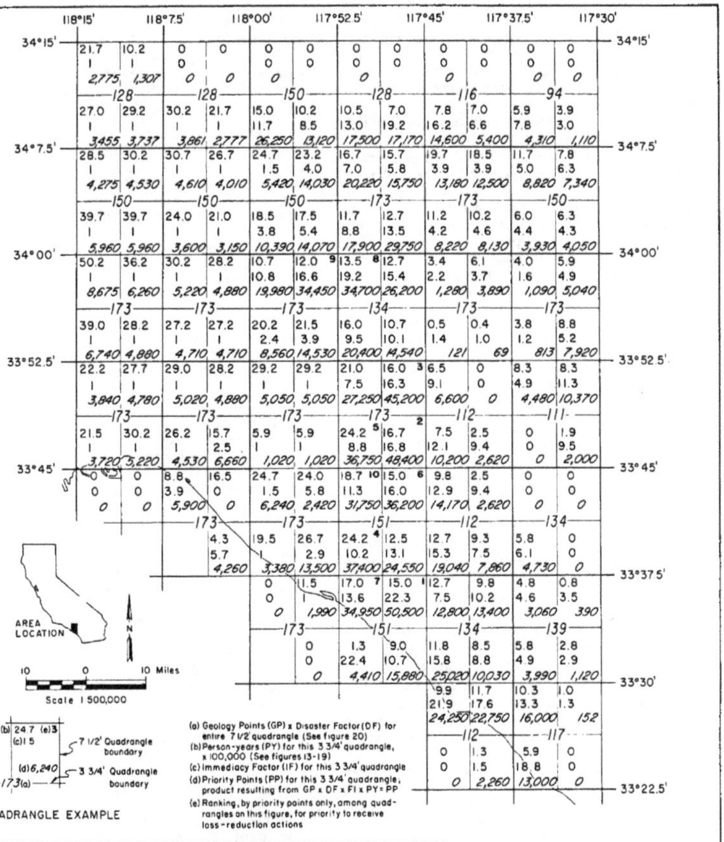

BASIC FORMULA:	GP (Geology Points)	x	DF (Disaster Factor)	x	IF (Immediacy Factor)	x	PY (Person-years)	=	PP (Priority Points)

GEOLOGY POINTS: Relative cumulative threat of loss in this quadrangle due to expectable damage from all geologic hazards present (See figure 20, and text section 5)

DISASTER FACTOR: Multiplier expressing major disruptive secondary effects of potentially catastrophic events that cause life-loss (See text section 5)

IMMEDIACY FACTOR: Relative timing of buildup of population density to "urban" condition in this quadrangle. Weighted to give higher priority to loss-reduction actions in quadrangles faced with earlier urbanization (See text, section 5)

PERSON-YEARS: Total number of persons expected to be living in this quadrangle during the period 1970-2000, multiplied by the number of years each will live in the quadrangle and be exposed to the various geologic hazards (See figures 13-19)

PRIORITY POINTS: Relative overall urgency for performing actions of all sorts to reduce losses from geologic hazards in this quadrangle (See text, section 5)

PRIORITY POINTS

(SAMPLE AREA, SELECTED TO SHOW METHODOLOGY)

CALIFORNIA DIVISION OF MINES AND GEOLOGY

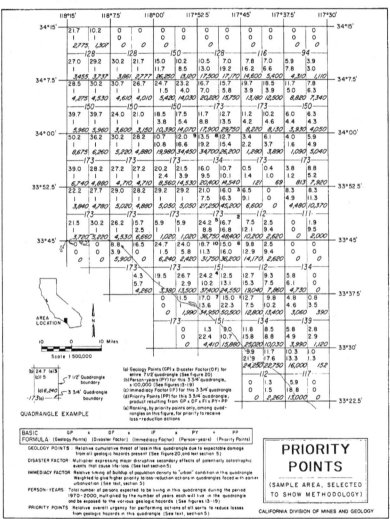

Figure 22. Priority Points. Sample area selected to show methodology.

should it be committed evenly among all the problems, or should the amount of expenditures be proportioned to the varied importance of the different problems? This is related to the traditional public budgeting decision—which functions should be emphasized? (e.g., education or social welfare or geologic safety?)

The results of this project indicate at least three independent approaches to this problem:

1. Ranking by total damage: The 10 geologic problems can be given priority ranking in the order of magnitude of damage they will cause over extended future time unless significant action is taken. Table 1, in Section 1, shows the projected total dollar loss from each problem in the 30-year period 1970–2000, if loss-reduction actions continue unchanged at their 1972 scope and level. The order of magnitude-of-loss listing is used throughout most of this report in discussing the 10 geologic problems:

Geologic problem	*Total loss, 1970–2000 ($ billion)*
1. Earthquake shaking	21
2. Loss of mineral resources	17
3. Landsliding	10
4. Flooding	6.5
5. Erosion activity	0.5
6. Expansive soils	0.15
7. Fault displacement	0.08
8. Volcanic hazards	0.05
9. Tsunami hazards	0.004
10. Subsidence	0.003

It is logical, in assigning priorities, to consider that those problems that offer the greatest total threat to the collective welfare deserve the most attention in the form of public agency loss-reduction programs.

2. Ranking by magnitude of possible loss-reduction: The 10 geologic problems can be given priority ranking in the order of the magnitude of the loss-reduction that can be achieved for each problem if 1972 loss-reduction measures are expanded significantly.

Table 1 (Section 1) also indicates (column 3) the dollar amounts by which the projected loss caused by each problem could be reduced over the 30 years 1970–2000, if all feasible loss-reduction measures were applied.

This ranking also suggests priority for overall concentration of public agency effort on those problems where the amount of public benefit stands to be largest. This ranking expresses the relative effectiveness of feasible loss-reduction measures.

Geologic problem	*Possible loss-reduction 1970–2000 ($ billion)*
1. Loss of mineral resources	15
2. Earthquake shaking	10
3. Landsliding	9
4. Flooding	3
5. Erosion activity	0.4
6. Expansive soils	0.15
7. Tsunami hazards	0.04
8. Subsidence	0.013
9. Fault displacement	0.013
10. Volcanic hazards	0.008

The priority logic of this ranking is also sound: Public expenditure should go first toward those problems that promise the most results.

3. Ranking by benefit:cost ratio: The ten geologic problems can be given priority ranking in the order of the benefit:cost ratios that can be achieved using available loss-reduction ratios.

Table 1 also indicates (column 5) the benefit:cost ratio of performing feasible loss-reduction measures for the 10 problems (costs), in terms of loss-reduction results (benefits) that would be obtained. This ranking reflects the relative efficiency of loss-reduction efforts spent on the several problems.

Geologic problem	Benefit:cost ratio
1. Loss of mineral resources	170:1
2. Expansive soils	20:1
3. Landsliding	9:1
4. Earthquake shaking	5:1
5. Volcanic hazards	5:1
6. Fault displacement	1.7:1
7. Subsidence	1.5:1
8. Tsunami hazards	1.5:1
9. Erosion activity	1.5:1
10. Flooding	1.3:1

The priority logic of this ranking also is sound: It is most efficient to concentrate expenditures where the public would get the most for its money.

In summary, this study has presented several valid approaches to help set priorities for concentrating or accelerating loss-reduction efforts on a single geologic problem, statewide. In practice, all of these approaches should be considered, in conjunction with other factors, since none of them clearly outweighs the others. However, it should be noted that earthquake shaking, loss of mineral resources, and landsliding are in the top three in the first two rankings and in the top four in the third ranking.

Priority Considerations by Loss-Reduction Programs

Many loss-reduction measures are available for attacking one or more of the several geologic problems, but shortage of resources to pursue all of them forces a priority selection as to which to emphasize. Given a particular locality that requires priority effort, or the particular problem(s) that need to be worked on in one locality or as a regional or statewide project, the main problem becomes "Exactly what action or actions should be taken first?"

In the long run, those actions that enable other actions must be completed first: the organizations who must perform basic research into the nature of each problem, or to advance the state of the art for coping with it, must press these responsibilities. Organizations that must adopt enabling statutes, or provide funds, or develop model language for ordinances, and like actions, must accomplish these things before other measures that depend on these actions can be taken.

In the short run, however, each of the many organizations with loss-reduction capability is faced with the responsibility of doing what it can do now, within existing limits of organization, means, and expertise. This has been the basic thrust of the recommendations in Section 4 of this report.

When faced with priority choices between programs for which it is equally capable, each organization should consciously favor priority for those of its programs that offer the most needed help to its ultimate constituency; that is, the citizens that select the legislative body that funds the organization and that select the executive officer or officers who, with their appointed officials, set administrative policy.

Hopefully, studies such as the Urban Geology Master Plan will help to place geologic problems in their proper context, both among each other and, taken as a whole, with other kinds of public problems. With this kind of information, program priorities can be determined on a rational basis.

Summary

Several principles regarding priority-setting have emerged in the course of this study.

1. The concept of "Geology Points" is helpful in guiding geotechnical agencies to localities and/or types of geologic problems that need their expertise. The specific Geology Point values arrived at in Phase I of this study are subject to improvement in areas where more detailed knowledge is available, especially where "no data" should be distinguished from "no danger" in assigning severity ratings.

2. Geology Points are most helpful when used to guide single agencies planning work programs to cope with specific geologic problems. The cumulative total Geology Points from all 10 problems indicate where total geologic hazards threats are highest in California, for general interest. But, for loss-reduction program planning, geotechnical organizations will be most helped by the Geology Points for just those problems with which they are concerned.

3. Priorities must be set essentially independently within each organization, at all levels of government and the private sector, to perform those actions within its capabilities. Program priority decisions must be made in the context of time and circumstances that prevail at the time the decision is made. Local governing bodies, with a given locality of responsibility and limited capabilities, must decide from local criteria which geologic problem to attack first, which loss-reduction measures to apply first, where in their jurisdiction to work first, and which action agency to assign to the task. Geotechnical agencies, also with fixed manpower, budget, capabilities, and expertise, and with limited mobility, must decide within those limitations which of their capabilities to emphasize, in which locality to work first, and which problem to tackle first.

4. Statewide and regional investigations of geologic problems in California are needed (a) to improve understanding of hazards processes and variables; (b) to locate and study regional problems that affect local uses but that can be studied best in off-site localities; (c) to develop the state of the art of detecting, evaluating, and overcoming problems; and (d) to provide data for regional decisions, such as the placement of utility and transportation lines.

5. The nature of the land-use decision process, in actual practice, is for the landowner to decide where he wants to place a given activity, largely ignoring potentially unfavorable geologic factors, then to take such engineering and structural measures as are required to make the site safe for the selected use. To serve this general practice of overcoming rather than avoiding geologic hazards, the types of geologic information collected, the degrees of detail required, the types of interpretation needed, and the methods of presentation should be designed to serve the engineer at least as well as the planner.

6. The definition of "undevelopable" localities should be kept very flexible, and geotechnical work should not be excluded from them without local consideration. Roads, buildings, and utility lines are often, of necessity, built on sites that are very unfavorable topographically and geologically, hopefully after engineering and structural measures have been taken to neutralize the natural geologic risk.

7. The most practical guideline as to where agency geologic work will be most useful is "Work in advance of population, in those areas expecting the largest and most immediate development." The concepts of "Person Years" and "Immediacy Factor," developed in Phase I of this study, are valid guidelines for planning priorities for geotechnical studies.

The overriding truth is that the collective geologic hazards problem in California is immense, and neither the knowledge nor the means are now available to do all that needs to be done if losses are to be reduced to the minimum level that is technologically possible.

This study has presented several approaches to guide the setting of priorities for loss-reduction work programs, but it is beyond its scope to dictate work-program priorities for other organizations to follow. The responsibility for making program-priority decisions remains with each organization involved in geologic problems, where the capability for making those decisions, based on its interpretation of the needs of its constituency belongs, along with the responsibility for conducting the needed programs.

Section 6

References and Bibliography

Referen

Adair, J. D., and Lungenc
earthquake hazard Lo
no. 4, pp. 155-163, Feb

Algermissen, S. T., Rine
James (1972) A stud
the San Francisco Bay
Dept. of Commerce, N
pheric Administration
oratories. A report prepa
gency Preparedness.

Brock, Leonard (19
port. City of Long Beac
23 p.

Bullard, F. M. (196
ory, in eruption. Univer

California Division of Mi
Urban Geology Master
1: A method for setting
72-24, ca. 500 p.

California Region Frame
(1971) Comprehensive
nia Region, Appendix IV
for the Pacific Southwest
Water Resources Counci

Castle, R. O., Yerkes, R. F.
A linear relationship be
and oil field subsidence
d'Hydrologie Scientif

Chesterman, C. W. (19
California Division of Mi
nia Geology, vol. 24,

Cluff, L. S., *et al.* (19
priority for geologic
ogy Master Plan for Ca
Division of Mines and
72-24.

Coffman, Jerry L. (1969
in the United States Co
Special Publication N

Corps of Engineers
study, California Regi
Engineer Division, S
630 Sansome Street, Sa
gust 1971.

Crumlish, J. D., and W
liminary study of
U. S. Coast and Ge
land.

Duke, C. Martin
earthquake. Keynote
quakes and their
Continuing education
University of California

Governor's Earthquake Com
port of the Governor

REFERENCES AND BIBLIOGRAPHY

References Cited

Adair, J. D., and Iungerich, R. (1972) Insuring the earthquake hazard. *Los Angeles Bar Bulletin*, vol. 47, no. 4, pp. 155–163, Feb. 1972.

Algermissen, S. T., Rinehart, W. A., and Dewey, James (1972) A study of earthquake losses in the San Francisco Bay area: Data and analysis. U. S. Dept. of Commerce, National Oceanic and Atmospheric Administraion, Environmental Research Laboratories. A report prepared for the Office of Emergency Preparedness, 220 p.

Brock, Leonard (1971) Fiscal 1970–71 Annual Report. City of Long Beach, Dept. of Oil Properties, 23 p.

Bullard, F. M. (1962) Volcanoes in history, in theory, in eruption. University of Texas Press, 441 p.

California Division of Mines and Geology (1971) Urban Geology Master Plan for California—Phase I: A method for setting priorities. Open-file report 72-24, ca. 500 p.

California Region Framework Study Committee (1971) Comprehensive Framework Study, California Region, Appendix IX—Flood Control. Prepared for the Pacific Southwest Inter-Agency Committee, Water Resources Council, June 1971.

Castle, R. O., Yerkes, R. F., and Riley, F. S. (1969) A linear relationship between liquid production and oil field subsidence. Association Internationale d'Hydrologie Scientifique.

Chesterman, C. W. (1971) Volcanism in California. California Division of Mines and Geology, *California Geology*, vol. 24, no. 8, pp. 139–147.

Cluff, L. S., *et al.* (1971) Methodology for setting priority for geologic investigations in Urban Geology Master Plan for California—Phase I. California Division of Mines and Geology open-file report 72-24.

Coffman, Jerry L. (1969) Earthquake investigations in the United States. Coast and Geodetic Survey Special Publication No. 282, revised edition, 57 p.

Corps of Engineers (1971) National shoreline study, California Regional inventory. U. S. Army Engineer Division, South Pacific, Corps of Engineers, 630 Sansome Street, San Francisco, California, August 1971.

Crumlish, J. D., and Wirth, G. F. (1967) A preliminary study of engineering seismology benefits. U. S. Coast and Geodetic Survey, Rockville, Maryland.

Duke, C. Martin (1971) The Great Los Angeles earthquake. Keynote talk for conference on earthquakes and their problems for a concerned citizenry. Continuing education in Engineering and Science, University of California Extension Los Angeles.

Governor's Earthquake Council (1972) First Report of the Governor's Earthquake Council, November 21, 1972. Available from the California Division of Mines and Geology, P.O. Box 2980, Sacramento, California 95812, for $1.50.

Hill, M. R. (1970) Mt. Lassen is in eruption and there is no mistake about that. California Division of Mines and Geology, *Mineral Information Service*, vol. 23, no. 11, pp. 211–224.

Hughes, Thomas H. (1971) Risks of earth movement and liability that result therefrom. *in* Joint Committee on Seismic Safety (see below, 1971a) p. 71–75.

James, David E. (1966) Geology and rock magnetism of Cinder Cone lava flows, Lassen Volcanic National Park, California. Geological Society of America Bulletin, vol. 77, no 3, p. 303–312.

Joint Committee on Seismic Safety (1971a) Earthquake risk, State of California. Joint Committee on Seismic Safety, 777 North First Street, Suite 600, San Jose, California 95112.

Joint Committee on Seismic Safety (1971b) The San Fernando earthquake of February 9, 1971 and public policy. State of California, Joint Committee on Seismic Safety, 777 North First Street, Suite 600, San Jose, California 95112.

Los Angeles County Earthquake Commission (1971) Report of the Los Angeles County Earthquake Commission, San Fernando Earthquake, February 9, 1971. 45 p.

McHarg, Ian (1969) Design with nature. American Museum of Natural History. Natural History Press, Garden City, N. Y. 11530.

Mirko, Francis C., and Stock, John A. (no date) The mineral industry of California, preprint from 1970 Minerals Yearbook, U. S. Bureau of Mines.

Mukerjee, Tapan (1972) The economics of optimal adjustments to earthquakes—I. Unpublished paper presented at the 4th Annual Conference of the Western Economics Association, Santa Clara, California, August 23–25, 1972. Available from the author at Department of Economics, University of the Pacific, Stockton, California 95204.

Radbruch, D. H., and Crowther, K. C. (1970) Map showing relative amounts of landslides in California. U. S. Geological Survey Open-File Report, 1970.

Tahoe Regional Planning Agency (no date) The plan for Lake Tahoe. Tahoe Regional Planning Agency, P. O. Box 8896, South Lake Tahoe, California 95705.

Taylor, F. A., and Brabb, E. E. (1972) Maps showing distribution and cost by counties of structurally damaging landslides in the San Francisco Bay region, California, winter of 1968–69. U. S. Geological Survey Map MF-327.

U. S. Coast and Geodetic Survey (1965) The story of the seismic sea-wave warning system. 46 p.

U. S. Forest Service (1971) Lake Tahoe Basin:

Planning for environmental quality. United States Forest Service, P.O. Box 8465, South Lake Tahoe, California 95705.

Weir, W. W. (1950) Subsidence of peat lands of the Sacramento-San Joaquin Delta, California. California University Agricultural Experiment Station, *Hilgardia*, vol. 20, no. 3, pp. 37–56.

Wood, H. O. and Heck, N. H. (1966) Earthquake history of the United States. Part II, Stronger earthquakes of California and western Nevada. U. S. Coast and Geodetic Survey, 48 p.

Yerkes, R. F. and Castle, R. O. (1969) Surface deformation associated with oil and gas field operations in the United States. Association d'Hydrologle Scientifique, Actes de Colloque de Tokyo, Affaissement de sol, pp. 55–66.

Selected Bibliography on Earthquake Shaking

Algermissen, S. T., Rinehart, W. A., and Dewey, James (1972) A study of earthquake losses in the San Francisco Bay area. A report prepared for the Office of Emergency Preparedness by the Environmental Research Laboratories of the National Oceanic and Atmospheric Administration, 220 p.

A series of scenarios describing effect of a future earthquake on various facilities for health care, utilities, and water storage.

Coffman, J. L. (1969) Earthquake investigations in the United States. Coast and Geodetic Survey Special Publication No. 282, revised edition, 57 p. Available from the Superintendent of Documents, Government Printing Office, Washington, D.C. 20402, for 35¢.

Iacopi, Robert (1964) Earthquake country. Lane Books, Menlo Park, California.

A non-technical presentation on faults, fault movement, and earthquake damage in California.

Los Angeles County Earthquake Commission (1971) Report of the Los Angeles County Earthquake Commission, San Fernando Earthquake, February 9, 1971.

Steinbrugge, K. V. (1968) Earthquake hazard in the San Francisco Bay Area: A continuing problem in public policy. Institute of Governmental Studies, University of California, Berkeley, California. $1.50.

Steinbrugge, K. V., chairman (1970) Earthquake hazard reduction. Executive Office of the President, Office of Science and Technology, Washington, D. C.

Steinbrugge, K. V., Schader, E. E., Bigglestone, H. C., and Weers, C. A. (1971) San Fernando earthquake, February 9, 1971. Insurance Services Office (formerly Pacific Fire Rating Bureau), 465 California Street, San Francisco, California.

Descriptions of losses to buildings and utilities.

Wiegel, R. L., editor (1970) Earthquake engineering. Prentice-Hall, Inc., Englewood Cliffs, New Jersey.

A source book with excellent papers and bibliographies.

Wood, H. O., and Heck, N. H. (1966) Earthquake history of the United States: Part II, Stronger earthquakes of California and western Nevada. Environmental Science Services Administration, Coast and Geodetic Survey. Available from the Superintendent of Documents, Washington, D. C. 20402, for 30¢.

A brief listing of earthquakes from 1769 to 1963.

Selected Bibliography on Loss of Mineral Resources

Cloud, Preston, chairman (1969) Resources and man. A study and recommendations by the Committee on Resources and Man, National Academy of Sciences — National Research Council. W. H. Freeman and Company, San Francisco, California.

Landerman, N. J., Schwartz, S., and Tapp, D. R. (1972) Community resource: the development-rehabilitation of sand and gravel lands. Southern California Rock Products Association, 1811 Fair Oaks, South Pasadena, California. $6.00.

A description of methods that can be used to protect, utilize and reclaim sand and gravel producing lands.

Park, C. F., Jr. (1968) Affluence in jeopardy—Minerals and the political economy. Freeman, Cooper and Co., San Francisco, California. 368 p.

The book discusses the dependence of our society on the availability of mineral resources. The first two chapters present a view of why known mineral deposits must be conserved through utilization.

Selected Bibliography on Landsliding

Cleaves, A. B. (1961) Landslide investigations. A field handbook for use in highway location and design. U. S. Department of Commerce, Bureau of Public Roads, 67 p. U. S. Government Printing Office, Washington, D. C. 20402, for 30¢.

A useful handbook describing kinds of landslides and methods of correcting them.

Highway Research Board (1958) Landslides and engineering practice. Highway Research Board, Special Report 29, 232 p.

A basic reference on landslides.

Slosson, J. E. (1969) The role of engineering geology in urban planning. The Governor's Conference on Environmental Geology, Colorado Geological Survey Special Publication No. 1, pp. 8–15.

Describes the record of improvement in landslide losses following enactment of the City of Los Angeles grading ordinance.

Taylor, F. A., and Brabb, E. E. (1972) Maps showing distribution and cost by counties of structurally damaging landslides in the San Francisco Bay Region, California, winter of 1968–69. U. S. Geological Survey Map MF-327.

Zaruba, Q. and Mencl, V. (1969) Landslides and their control. Elsevier Press, Amsterdam, 205 p.

Selected Bibliography on Flooding

California Region Framework Study Committee (1971) Comprehensive Framework Study, California Region, Appendix IX—Flood Control. Prepared for the Pacific Southwest Inter-Agency Committee, Water Resources Council, June 1971.

Selected Bibliography on Erosion Activity

Powell, M. D., Winter, W. C., and Bowditch, W. P. (1970) Community Action guidebook for soil erosion and sediment control. National Association of Counties Research Foundation, 1001 Connecticut Avenue, N.W., Washington, D. C. 20036.

Selected Bibliography on Expansive Soils

Portland Cement Association (no date) Recommended practice for construction of residential concrete floors on expansive soils. Volume II available from the Association for $2.63 at 520 S. LaFayette Park Place, Los Angeles, California 90057.

A general but useful handbook describing methods of testing for expansive soil, treatment of soils, and foundation design.

Selected Bibliography on Fault Displacement

Cluff, L. S. (1968) Urban development within the San Andreas fault system. Proceedings of Conference on Geologic Problems of San Andreas Fault System, Stanford University Publications in the Geological Sciences, vol. XI, pp. 55–69.

Cluff, L. S., Slemmons, D. B., and Waggoner, E. B. (1970) Active fault zone hazards and related problems of siting works of man. Proceedings of the Fourth Symposium on Earthquake Engineering, University of Roorkee, India.

Mader, G. G., Danehy, E. A., Cummings, J. C., and Dickinson, W. R. (1972) Land use restrictions along the San Andreas fault in Portola Valley, California. Proceedings of the International Conference on Microzonation for Safer Construction, Research and Application, University of Washington, Seattle, Washington.

Slemmons, D. B. (1972) Microzonation for surface faulting. Proceedings of the International Conference on Microzonation for Safer Construction, Research and Application, University of Washington, Seattle, Washington.

All of these articles discuss the need for setback distances from active faults and give some examples.

Selected Bibliography on Volcanic Hazards

Bullard, F. M. (1962) Volcanoes in history, in theory, in eruption. University of Texas Press, 441 p.

Chesterman, C. W. (1971) Volcanism in California. *California Geology*, vol. 24, no. 8, pp. 139–147, August 1971.

Crandell, D. R. and Mullineaux, D. R. (1967) Volcanic hazards at Mount Rainier, Washington. U. S. Geological Survey Bulletin 1238.

Crandell, D. R. and Waldron, H. (1969) Volcanic hazards in the Cascade Range. Geologic Hazards and Public Problems, Office of Emergency Preparedness, pp. 5–18. Available from the Superintendent of Documents, Washington, D.C. 20402, for $2.75.

Hill, M. R. (1970) Mt. Lassen is in eruption and there is no mistake about that. *Mineral Information Service*, vol. 23, no. 11, pp. 211–224, November 1970.

Waldron, H. H. (1967) Debris flow and erosion control problems caused by the ash eruptions of Irazu Volcano, Costa Rica. U. S. Geological Survey Bulletin 1241-I.

Contains descriptions of the types of damage resulting from an ash eruption similar to those that have happened in California.

Selected Bibliography on Tsunami Hazards

Heck, N. H. (1947) List of seismic sea waves. *Bulletin* of the Seismological Society of America, vol. 37, no. 4, pp. 269–286.

The author describes 270 tsunamis through 1947 but considers the list to be incomplete due to lack of information.

U. S. Coast and Geodetic Survey (1965) The story of the seismic sea-wave warning system. 46 p.

Wiegel, R. L. (1964) Oceanographical engineering. Prentice-Hall Inc., Englewood Cliffs, New Jersey, 532 p.

Wiegel, R. L. (1970) Tsunamis. Chapter II *in* Earthquake engineering, Prentice-Hall Inc., Englewood Cliffs, New Jersey, pp. 253–306.

Wood, H. O., and Heck, N. H. (1966) Earthquake history of the United States. Part II, Stronger earthquakes of California and Western Nevada. U. S. Coast and Geodetic Survey, 48 p.

Selected Bibliography on Subsidence

Castle, R. O., Yerkes, R. F., and Riley, F. S. (1969) A linear relationship between liquid production and oil field subsidence. Association Internationale d'Hydrologie Scientifique.

Lofgren, Ben (1965) Subsidence related to ground water withdrawal. *In* Landslides and Subsidence—Record of proceedings of conference sponsored by The Resources Agency of California, pp. 105–110. Available from the California Division of Mines and Geology, P.O. Box 2980, Sacramento, California 95812, for $1.00.

Lucas, Cliff (1965) Shallow subsidence studies for the California Aqueduct. Landslides and Subsidence—Record of proceedings of conference sponsored by The Resources Agency of California, pp. 111–116. Available from the California Division of Mines and Geology, P.O. Box 2980, Sacramento, California 95812, for $1.00.

Mayuga, M. N. (1965) How subsidence affects the City of Long Beach. *In* Landslides and Subsidence—Record of proceedings of conference sponsored by The Resources Agency of California, pp. 122–129. Available from the California Division of Mines and Geology, P.O. Box 2980, Sacramento, California 95812, for $1.00.

Weir, W. W. (1950) Subsidence of peat lands of the Sacramento-San Joaquin Delta, California. California University Agricultural Experiment Station, *Hilgardia,* vol. 20, no. 3, pp. 37–56.

Yerkes, R. F. and Castle, R. O. (1969) Surface deformation associated with oil and gas field operations in the United States. Association d'Hydrologie Scientifique, Actes de Colloque de Tokyo, Affaissement de Sol, pp. 55–66.

Section 7

Appendices A B and C

A basic factor in the
(UGMP) project is the
geologic problem, main
life-loss and injury. T
total expectable losses
year period 1970-2000
Points" (Section 5) als
determined to indicate
loss in the several seve
in dollars per person p

Loss data for geolo
mentary and inconsiste
for most geologic prob
only isolated example
to extrapolation, comb
lar-loss data have been
of different events of th
earthquakes) varying w
pose of the data collect
stronger when losses are
kinds of geologic prob
as to apportionment be
earthquake shaking and
merge; flood loss figure
landslide data.

Faced with these limi
and reliability of availab
ogy Master Plan project
mated figures for annua
loss totals using the best

The Phase I study (Cal
Geology, 1971) develope
thetical "urban unit"—
area of about one-third of
lation of 3000. The magn
lem was derived by hypo
unit in the various severi
simulating the amounts of
cur over a representative
Geology Points was obta
Mines and Geology, 19

During Phase II of the U
ments were made of the Ph
particular dollar values fo
adjustment in comparison
veloped during this proce
areas. Most of the Phase I p
fied significantly, as were
able annual and 30-year pro

The main rationale, assum
used to obtain the Geology P
in the Urban Geology Master
this Appendix.

APPENDIX A

Costs of Losses and Loss-Reduction Measures

A basic factor in the Urban Geology Master Plan (UGMP) project is the magnitude of loss from each geologic problem, mainly from property damage and life-loss and injury. Table 1 (Section 1) summarizes total expectable losses, as extended totals for the 30-year period 1970–2000. The priority factor "Geology Points" (Section 5) also requires that dollar values be determined to indicate the magnitude of expectable loss in the several severity zones for each problem, in dollars per person per year.

Loss data for geologic problems are at best fragmentary and inconsistent in the available literature; for most geologic problems the historic data provide only isolated examples which are often poorly suited to extrapolation, combination, or generalization. Dollar-loss data have been collected for different aspects of different events of the same problems (e.g., various earthquakes) varying with time and place, and purpose of the data collectors. The inconsistency is even stronger when losses are compared between different kinds of geologic problems. Many data are blurred as to apportionment between related problems: e.g., earthquake shaking and fault-displacement loss data merge; flood loss figures often include erosion and landslide data.

Faced with these limitations on the type, format, and reliability of available loss data, the Urban Geology Master Plan project was forced to develop estimated figures for annual expectable loss and 30-year loss totals using the best means available.

The Phase I study (California Division of Mines and Geology, 1971) developed the concept of a hypothetical "urban unit"—a typically developed urban area of about one-third of a square mile, with a population of 3000. The magnitude of loss from each problem was derived by hypothetically placing the urban unit in the various severity zones of each problem. By simulating the amounts of damage-loss that would occur over a representative time interval, a trial set of Geology Points was obtained (California Division of Mines and Geology, 1971, table 3-23).

During Phase II of the UGMP study, many refinements were made of the Phase I rationale, method, and particular dollar values for each problem, mainly by adjustment in comparison with case histories developed during this project by study of five local areas. Most of the Phase I geology points were modified significantly, as were their extensions into expectable annual and 30-year loss totals.

The main rationale, assumptions, and calculations used to obtain the Geology Points and loss figures used in the Urban Geology Master Plan are summarized in this Appendix.

EVALUATION OF EARTHQUAKE SHAKING LOSSES

Based on earthquake-shaking losses actually experienced in the several quadrangles analyzed in detail during Phase II of the UGMP study, the following values were reached, showing the expectable average per capita annual loss, in dollars, to each resident of the severity zone in question:

Earthquake shaking severity zone	Property damage component (one-half public sector one-half private sec or)[1]		Intangible loss component[1]		Life-loss and injury component[1]		Geology Points (expectable total average loss rate)[1]
High	14	+	14	+	3	=	31
Moderate	13	+	13	+	1	=	27
Low	7	+	7	+	0	=	14

[1] Average cost per person living in this severity zone, per year, in dollars.

Statewide totals to the year 2000 were obtained: (1) for expected losses at 1970 levels of loss-reduction; (2) for the amount by which that loss could possibly be reduced; and (3) for the amount such loss-reduction efforts would cost. (See Section 1, table 1). The 30-year total loss was estimated by multiplying the expectable per capita per year dollar loss times the total number of people expected to be in the quadrangles of each severity zone between 1970 and 2000.

If 1972 state-of-the-art techniques for reducing the losses due to earthquake shaking were applied to the fullest degree feasible over the period 1970 to 2000, earthquake dollar loss is estimated to be reducible by 50 percent. Of this total reduction, engineering seismology measures should reduce the loss by 41 percent (Crumlish and Wirth, 1967, p. 36–37), and all other measures should reduce the loss by an additional 9 percent.

$$50\% \times \$21,035,000,000 = \$10,517,500,000$$

Based on experience and data gathered in selected areas during Phase II of this study, feasible loss reduction measures should cost 10 percent of total loss.

$$10\% \times \$21,035,000,000 = \$2,103,500,000$$

Combined, these figures indicate a benefit:cost ratio of 5:1 ($10,517,500,000:$2,103,500,000), which argues strongly in terms of economics, for implementing effective earthquake reduction measures. In addition to

Earthquake severity zone[1]	Number of urban 7½ minute quadrangles of each severity	Estimated percent of total population[2]	Estimated person-years exposure 1970–2000	Geology Points (expectable total average loss rate) (dollars per capita per year)	Projected total loss 1970–2000
High	181	37½	289,050,000	31	$9,280,000,000
Moderate	242	50	385,400,000	27	10,406,000,000
Low	57	12½	96,350,000	14	1,349,000,000
			770,800,000		$21,035,000,000

[1] Three degrees of estimated earthquake severity in California (California Division of Mines and Geology, 1971, fig. 3–4; p. 312–322).
[2] Total population (person-years) in California for 30-year period 1970–2000 from Livingston and Blayney's population projections (California Division of Mines and Geology, 1971, p. 5-1 to 5-11).

the needs for increased public safety and the social and political concerns therefor, earthquake safety, on balance, is also "good business".

EVALUATION OF LOSSES OF MINERAL RESOURCES (DUE TO URBANIZATION)

The Geology Points (California Division of Mines and Geology 1971, p. 3–59) for Loss of Mineral Resources were changed from the Phase I value of $44 to $22 during the Phase II analysis on the basis of the following rationale. The loss of mineral resources due to urban development is taken as the increase in cost of minerals to each California resident due to the increased haul distance. The main mineral resources that are in conflict with urbanization pressures in California are the common construction materials—sand and gravel, cement, clay, and stone products. The tonnage of these materials produced (and consumed) in California in 1970 is about 200,000,000 tons, valued at about $2.20 per ton (Mitko and Stock, no date, p. 2). For the 1970 population of about 20,000,000, consumption averages 10 tons per capita per year. For the projected population of about 34,000,000 at year 2000 (California Division of Mines and Geology, 1971, table 5-1), the projected consumption of about 400,000,000 tons of these minerals (U.S. Bureau of Mines, written communication, January 22, 1971) will amount to 12 tons average annual consumption per capita.

In 1970 the average haulage distance for these materials is estimated to be about 25 miles, whereas by 2000 more distant deposits will be in use, requiring an estimated average haulage distance of about 50 miles.

In 1970 the cost of haulage is about $0.04 per ton-mile, but by 2000 it is estimated that this will increase to about $0.09 per ton-mile.

Thus, in 1970 the average annual per capita cost of hauling mineral materials was $10, whereas by 2000 it will have jumped to an estimated $54 as shown in the calculations below. The $44 difference in the annual per capita haulage cost represents the added cost to every California resident due to the near-market deposits being lost to use because of urbanization pressures.

	Average haulage distance in miles		Average cost per ton-mile		Average annual per capita consumption in tons		Average annual per capita cost of hauling
1970	25	×	$0.04	×	10	=	$10
2000	50	×	$0.09	×	12	=	$54

The Geology Points for loss of mineral resources are thus one-half of 44, or 22, corresponding to the average additional per capita cost of haulage for the 30-year period, 1970 to 2000. No life loss and injury cost or disaster factor are involved.

Statewide total loss, if 1972 practice regarding saving mineral deposits from losses due to urbanization were to continue unchanged, is estimated by multiplying the expectable average loss rate for the 30-year period ($22 per capita per year) by the total population of California 1970 to 2000, in person years (California Division of Mines and Geology, 1971, p. 5-1 to 5-11):

$22 × 770,800,000 = $16,957,600,000 total expectable 30-year loss in California

That loss could be reduced by an estimated 90 percent ($15 billion) if methods known and available in 1972 were to be rigorously applied: identify those deposits that lie in the path of urbanization, and place them in zones to protect them and their processing plants and access routes until they are worked out.

The cost of these loss-prevention practices would be about $90 million: an estimated average of 30 man-years of local government zoning effort per county, and 30 man-years of mineral resources specialist effort per county in the period 1970–2000. Required personnel may be full-time, part-time, or short-term, and either public employees or consultants. The necessary effort in each city or county will vary from near-zero to several man-years. It should be stressed that these average figures are used only for purposes of arriving at an estimated total statewide cost.

The benefit : cost ratio would be about 170 :1.

EVALUATION OF LANDSLIDE LOSSES

Geology Point values, to indicate the relative threat of damage from landslides and other slope instability phenomena, are based on intensive analyses of selected areas during Phase II of this study.

The expectable loss per capita per year in Landslide —high severity zones (California Division of Mines and

Landslide severity zone	Number of urban quadrang es of each severity	Estimated percent of total population	Person-years exposure (to year 2000)	Geology Points (expectable total loss rate) (dollars per capita per year)	Projected total loss 1970–2000
High	200	7	53 956,000	53	$2,859,000,000
Moderate	700	25	192,700,000	35	6,745,000,000
Low	900	32	246,656,000	1	247,000,000
					$9,851,000,000

Geology, 1971, figure 3-11) under 1972 loss-reduction practice, averages about $53 for all physical and intangible damage loss. Life loss and injury loss from landslides has been negligible, but since life can be lost, a disaster factor of 1.1 has been used. The $53 expectable loss is a mean between loss figures from several typical high severity landslide areas where loss-reduction measures are being applied quite differently. For example, in parts of Orange County, where 1972 state-of-the-art measures are routinely applied, the expectable loss per person per year is about $3.30; in comparable landslide-prone localities in other regions where relatively little is being done to prevent losses, the corresponding loss figure is about $104 per capita per year. For Landslide—moderate severity zones, an estimate of two-thirds the high severity threat level is used, or $35 per capita per year. In Landslide—low severity zones, an arbitrary minimum loss figure is used: $1 per capita per year.

Statewide totals to the year 2000 were projected: (1) for expectable overall losses if 1972 practices of loss-reduction continue unchanged; (2) for the amount by which that loss could possibly be reduced if all 1972 state-of-the-art landslide loss-reduction measures were rigorously applied; and (3) for the amount that such application of loss-reduction measures would cost. (See Section 1, table 1).

The 30-year total loss is estimated to be $9,852,000,000, arrived at by multiplying the expectable per capita per year dollar loss times the total number of people projected to be in the quadrangles of each severity zone between 1970 and 2000.

The possible reduction of that 30-year loss if all measures available in 1972 are applied rigorously, is estimated to be 90 percent, or $8,865,000,000.

The cost of applying 1972 state-of-the-art loss-prevention measures was determined to average $4.70 per capita per year for those living in the hillside areas studied during Phase II of this project, and the benefit: cost ratio to be 8.7:1. Applying this ratio to the possible "benefit" of $8,865,000,000 that can be saved, we obtain the figure $1,018,000,000 for the 30-year cost of applying those measures.

EVALUATION OF FLOODING LOSSES

To calculate Geology Points for the complicated threats of flood hazards to urban areas requires large-scale flood-potential maps that show local drainage problems, as well as river runoff overflow areas. Flood-control dams and levee systems should be shown, too, and designed overflow bypasses should be distinguished from planned dry areas.

The Geology Points (California Division of Mines and Geology, 1971, p. 3-23 to 3-25) for Flooding—high severity ($127 damage loss, plus $7.50 life loss, for total $134.50 loss per capita per year—hence Geology Point value of $134.50) apply to major river flood areas, but not to the minor streams and designed bypasses also shown as "flood hazard areas" on figure 3-7 of that report.

Flooding—moderate severity value, estimated to be ⅓ of the high severity value, applies to areas threatened by minor stream overflows and local drainage flooding.

The Phase I Geology Point values need two-fold modification to allow for intangible losses, and 4.8-fold increase in the life-loss and injury value, as determined in the Phase II analysis, as follows:

Geology Points for flooding are:

Flooding severity zone	Property damage component (one-half public sector, one-half private sector)[1]		Intangible loss component[1]		Life-loss and injury component[1]		Geology Points (expectable average annual loss-rate)[1]
High	127	+	127	+	36	=	290
Moderate	42	+	42	+	12	=	96

[1] Average costs per person living in this severity zone, per year, in dollars.

Projected statewide flood losses, 1970 to 2000, were adjusted in proportion to that time interval from data developed by California Region Framework Study Committee (1971, pages 9–20). According to the Framework Study Committee, if the 1965 type and extent of flood prevention and flood control measures are maintained until the year 2000 without change, the total statewide loss due to flooding would total $6,532,000,000.

If all feasible flood loss-reduction measures available in 1970 and recommended in the Framework Study were put into effect, the 30-year loss could be reduced by $3,432,000,000 (52%) to $3,100,000,000, according to that study.

The estimated cost of installation and operation of the measures recommended by the Framework Study for the 30-year period is $2,703,000,000, for a benefit: cost ratio of about 1.3:1.

EVALUATION OF EROSION LOSSES

Estimates of erosion loss are based partly on the differential natural propensity of California soils to erosion (California Division of Mines and Geology, 1971, p. 3-46 to 3-49), and partly on analysis during Phase II of this study. Data on coastal erosion is taken from the U.S. Army Corps of Engineers, "National Shoreline Study—California Regional Inventory" (1971, ca. 220 pages).

Geology Points, indicating the expectable annual average dollar loss due to erosion per person in the several erosion severity zones in California, are based on the erosion potential of undisturbed areas, recognizing soil profile type, natural vegetation, and slope of natural surface (California Division of Mines and Geology, 1971, fig. 3-13). The Phase I estimates of expectable dollar loss (California Division of Mines and Geology, 1971, page 3-47, and figure 3-13) (Erosion activity—high severity: $1.50;—moderate severity: $1.11; and—low severity: $0.36) are doubled to account for inherent intangible costs as determined in Phase II of this study, and rounded to yield these Geology Points: (life-loss and injury, and disaster factor are both nil.)

Erosion loss—high severity : 3
—moderate severity: 2
—low severity : 1

Unfortunately these Geology Points do not account for the very substantial costs (estimated $6 million per year in California) of coastal erosion (figure 3-13 in California Division of Mines and Geology, 1971, does not indicate its threat). Further, they do not reflect the fact that the urbanization process tends to modify the undisturbed surface materials, and the resulting erosion effects, in unpredictable ways: soil profiles are homogenized by bulldozers, vegetation is destroyed or replaced, and natural slope and local drainage are variously altered.

Statewide loss estimations, assuming that 1972 level and type of loss-reduction actions continue for 30 years unchanged, are arrived at as follows. Recognizing that both theoretically and practically, "erosion" damage, erosion-preventive actions, and erosion-damage cleanup actions are inextricably intermingled with the damages, actions and costs commonly labeled "flooding" and "landsliding", 1/50 of flood and landslide damage has been arbitrarily selected as "erosion":

(Flooding):	1/50 × $4,230,000,000	=	$84,600,000
(Landsliding):	1/50 × 9,850,000,000	=	197,000,000
			$281 600,000 (1970–2000)

Erosion damage to roadbeds and other structures public and private (although damage suffered by private landowners is largely undeclared), is estimated at $50,000 per county per year, or $90,000,000 (1970–2000).

Cleanup of erosion debris is estimated to cost about $25,000 per county per year, or $45,000,000 (1970–2000).

Coastal erosion will result in losses costing an estimated $148,500,000 over the 30 years to 2000. This is estimated as follows:

a) The Corps of Engineers (1971, p. 109) estimates $99,000,000 cost, to year 2000, of the projects they recommend as needed.

b) In their benefit:cost determinations, the Corps of Engineers uses the ratio of 1:1 to determine feasibility. Therefore the benefits of the needed work are estimated to equal the proposed cost: $99,000,000.

c) The proposed projects will not reduce losses to zero, but will still leave an estimated ⅓ of the loss as an unavoidable residual. The loss even after the projects are done will still be about $50,000,000; but if nothing were done, the estimated total loss over the next 30 years would be about $148,500,000.

So total loss due to all forms of erosion to year 2000, if 1972 loss-reduction practices remain unchanged in type and degree, will be on the order of $565,000,000.

Loss reduction, assuming that ⅔ of that total loss can be prevented by rigorously applying all feasible loss-reduction measures over the next 30 years, would be $377,000,000.

Costs of this estimated 30-year erosion prevention and control program would include 1/50 of the costs of flooding and landslide loss prevention (1/50 × $265,000,000) or $5,300,000 for flooding, plus (1/50 × $1,018,000,000) or $20,360,000 for landsliding.

The 30-year program costs would also include an estimated $121,800,000 for increased grading and engineering works (estimated $70,000 per year, in 58 counties, over 30 years); and $99,000,000 for coastal erosion measures.

Total estimated costs are $247,000,000. The benefit:cost ratio would be $377,000,000:$247,000,000, or about 1.5:1.

EVALUATION OF LOSSES DUE TO EXPANSIVE SOILS

Geology Points, indicating the expected annual average dollar loss per person living in areas subject to damage from expansive soil, are based on analyses of actual experience in representative localities, during Phase II of this project. For Expansive soils—high severity zones, the expectable per capita per year loss is $2.52; with life-loss and injury costs and disaster factor both nil, the Geology Points figure rounds out to 3. The same investigations and reasoning suggests a Geology Point figure for Expansive soils—moderate severity zones of about 2, and for low severity zones, nil.

Because the available maps showing distribution of expansive soils (California Division of Mines and Geology, 1971, figure 3-14) are too generalized to use directly with the Geology Point values to obtain statewide totals, another approach was required. The equivalent, estimated, of some 500 structures including buildings, roads, airports, etc., are damaged in California each year by expansive soils, by an amount estimated at $10,000 each. This yields an estimated 30-year total damage, if 1972 procedures are continued unchanged, of $150,000,000.

That loss could be reduced almost completely if known and available loss-reduction methods were applied rigorously over the next 30 years to all building sites with expansive soils; at an assumed 99 percent effectiveness, the loss reduction would be $148,500,000. These methods would cost an estimated average of $500 per structure, or $7,500,000, and the benefit:cost ratio would be about 20:1.

EVALUATION OF FAULT DISPLACEMENT LOSSES

The Geology Points developed in Phase I (California Division of Mines and Geology, 1971, p. 3-35 to 3-37) representing per capita per year losses from fault displacement (Fault displacement—high severity: 9.00;—moderate severity: 0.09; and—low severity: 0.002) were modified during Phase II of this project. The recurrence rate estimated in Phase I of this project for damaging fault movement in California was reduced ⅘ to one movement every 5 years, to meet experience after the San Fernando earthquake of 1971 and other fault movement events. The estimated dollar loss per damaging fault movement was decreased ⅔, from $1,880,000 to $620,000 on the basis of what is known about fault damage loss in California. The life loss per fault movement was decreased ¾ from 12 deaths every event to 3 on the basis of experience in actual California fault movement losses. On the other hand, the new life-loss and injury figure of $360,000 per life loss (4.8 times the $75,000 per death used in California Division of Mines and Geology, 1971) increases the expectable loss; the physical damage value was doubled to allow for concomitant intangible (non-structural, socio-economic) loss as determined from a study of a local area in the San Fernando Valley; and a disaster factor of 1.1 was introduced, applying to Fault displacement high severity.

A decreasing recurrence interval is the only variable between high, moderate, and low severity zones of fault displacement. A 1000-year recurrence interval is estimated for prehistoric Quaternary faults (moderate severity zone), reducing the Geology Points to 0.5 (rounded to 1 to keep whole numbers) for Fault displacement—moderate. Similarly, the recurrence interval for damaging movement of pre-Quaternary (low severity) faults is estimated to be 10,000 years reducing the Geology Points for Fault displacement—low severity to nil.

Geology Points for fault displacement are:

Fault displacement severity zone	Property damage component (one-half public sector, one-half private sector)[1]		Intangible loss component[1]		Life loss and injury component[1]		Geology Points (expectable average annual loss rate)[1]
High........	.60	+	.60	+	3.75	=	5
Moderate....	.06	+	.06	+	0.38	=	1
Low.........	.01	+	.01	+	.04	=	0

[1] Average costs per person living in this severity zone, per year, in dollars.

Statewide totals to the year 2000 for expected losses if 1972 levels of loss reduction continue unchanged are based on projections developed in Phase II studies.

As of 1970, an estimated 1,300 private and 250 public structures have been built astride active faults that have an estimated recurrence interval of 100 years. Over the next 30 years, by 2000, an estimated additional 520 private structures—residential and commercial—and 130 more public structures will be built astride active faults, if present practice continues. Assuming that 30 percent of the 100-year recurrence faults will move during the next 30 years, 30 percent of the now existing structures and 15 percent of those yet to be built will be damaged during that time interval. At the assumed average cost of $40,000 per private structure damaged, private structural losses will total $19,000,000; at the assumed average cost of $200,000 per public structure damaged, the corresponding loss to the public sector will also be $19,000,000, for a total tangible loss of $38,000,000.

Adding an equal amount for assumed non-structural, socio-economic losses, we get a grand total projected loss due to fault displacement in California of $76,000,000 for the period 1970–2000.

The hundreds of structures already built on active faults cannot be made safe from fault displacement, but by avoiding any further construction on known active faults, it is possible to save an estimated 85 percent of the 105 new structures both public and private that otherwise would be built and damaged before 2000, for a loss-reduction of about $12,600,000—$6.3 million tangible, and $6.3 million non-structural, socio-economic.

The cost of future loss-reduction measures lies mainly in site investigations, which for practical purposes may be considered in two steps:

1. Preliminary or general investigations, to determine the general localities where active faults are believed to exist and fault displacement damage is considered to be a potential danger.
2. Final, or detailed investigations of all proposed building sites within the potential fault-displacement zones delineated in the preliminary investigations. The detailed investigation is to determine whether an active fault really

exists within the designated locality, and if so, to pinpoint its position, including possible laterals and offshoots.

The preliminary type of fault investigations, such as the California Division of Mines and Geology mapping of special studies zones along the traces of major active faults under Chapter 7.5, Division 2, Public Resources Code (Alquist-Priolo Geologic Hazard Zones Act) are relatively low in cost per building site. In the thirty-year period from 1970 to 2000 such studies will cost an estimated $80,000 per year, or about $2,375,000 total.

Detailed fault investigations, required only in the limited areas delineated as special studies zones, require intensive field study, usually including trenching, and are much more expensive per building site. Detailed investigations of residential building sites cost an estimated average of $200 per site; detailed investigations of public structure building sites cost an estimated average of $5,000 per site, but may be much higher for major structures like dams or bridges.

If one out of three detailed fault investigations results in preventing construction on an active fault, the cost of these investigations per private structure saved would be $600, and $15,000 per public structure saved. Applied to the numbers of buildings projected to be built where active faults will damage them during the period 1970–2000, and assuming 85 percent of these potential losses would be prevented, the total costs of detailed fault investigations to year 2000 will be about $2,000,000—about $300,000 total for private building site studies, and about $1,700,000 total for public construction sites.

If we assume these investigations reduce the land value by $5,000 at each of the 552 sites where construction is prevented, due to restrictions on building, the additional "loss" to property values would total about $2,500,000.

The total costs of these programs for reducing fault displacement losses in California, 1970 to 2000, are approximately $7,500,000.

The indicated benefit:cost ratio on applying these measures is about $12.6 million:$7.5 million, or about 2:1.

EVALUATION OF VOLCANIC HAZARDS LOSSES

Volcanic hazards are unique among the problems treated in this document in that their threats are primarily outside the state's urban areas. Therefore this analysis of potential losses and loss-reduction measures is on a "whole-state" basis with respect to such things as estimated population data, and land and improvement values.

The Phase I Geology Points (California Division of Mines and Geology, 1971, p. 3-29), Volcanic hazards—high: 400;—moderate: 6; and—low: 0.06 were modified during Phase II studies to a lower recurrence rate of damaging eruptions, fewer people in areas actually threatened, smaller areas destroyed per event, and lower value to property destroyed; but to a higher value for life lost and a much closer degree of damage between high, moderate, and low severity zones.

The resulting Geology Points are:

Volcanic hazards severity zone	Property damage component (one-half public sector, one-half private sector)[1]		Intangible loss component[1]		Life-loss and injury component[1]		Geology Points (expectable average annual loss-rate)[1]
High	4.50	+	4.50	+	48	=	57
Moderate	2.75	+	2.75	+	4.80	=	10
Low	1.00	+	1.00	+	1.00	=	3

[1] Average costs per person living in this severity zone, per year, in dollars.

Statewide totals to the year 2000 were projected for: (1) expectable overall losses if 1972 practices of loss reduction continue unchanged; (2) the amount by which that loss could possibly be reduced if all 1972 state-of-the-art loss-prevention measures were rigorously applied; and (3) the amount that such application of loss-reduction measures would cost (See Section 1, table 1.)

The 30-year total loss is estimated to be $49,380,000, derived by multiplying the expectable annual per capita dollar loss times the total number of people projected to be in the quadrangles of each severity zone between 1970 and 2000.

Volcanic hazards severity zone	Number of quadrangles of each severity	Estimated person-years exposure 1970–2000	Geology Points (expectable total average loss rate) (dollars per capita per year)	Projected total loss 1970–2000
High	21	315,000	57	$17,955,000
Medium	115	1,725,000	10	17,250,000
Low	315	4,725,000	3	14,175,000
				$49,380,000

Possible reduction of that loss is estimated to be $8,135,000, obtained by estimating 25 percent of tangible property value and 50 percent of life loss and injury costs could be saved if all measures known and available in 1972 were to be rigorously applied.

The costs of applying that loss-reduction effort (improved advance warning of events, improved recognition of local dangers, improved communications and planning) would total an estimated $1,655,000 for the 30-year period. The benefit:cost ratio would be about 5:1.

Subsidence severity zone	Number of urban 7½-minute quadrangles of each severity	Estimated percent of total population[1]	Estimated person-years exposure 1970–2000	Geology Points (expectable total average loss-rate) (dollars per capita per year)	Projected total loss 1970–2000
High..........................	196	7	53,956,000	0.34	$18,345,000
Low..........................	1,453	52	400,816,000	0.02	8,016,000
					$26,361,000

[1] Total person-years in California 1970–2000 projected to be 770,800,000.

EVALUATION OF TSUNAMI HAZARDS LOSSES

Tsunami threat is unique among the geologic problems being considered in this Urban Geology Master Plan in that it exists only along seacoasts and even there only at a few well identified localities. Therefore, the concept of Geology Points as an indicator of loss to the average citizen of coastal quadrangle must be modified: a more concentrated threat applies to inhabitants of the actual coastal strip, and none to the backshore inhabitants of the coastal quadrangles, or to any inland quadrangles. The considerable threat of damage to floating vessels must be dispersed among owners who may live unknown miles away.

The Phase I Geology Points (California Division of Mines and Geology, 1971, p. 3-34)—Tsunami hazard —high severity: 69;—moderate severity: 0.41;—low severity: 0.03—are modified in accordance with Phase II analysis of tsunami threat, as follows:

Crescent City is the only California locality to require a tsunami—high severity factor, which corresponds to $216. This value is arrived at by doubling the Phase I physical damage to account for non-structural socio-economic losses; increasing the Phase I life-loss and injury figure from $75,000 to $360,000 per life lost; and applying a disaster factor of 1.5.

Tsunami—moderate severity factor applies to all harbor areas other than Crescent City, and to vulnerable localities on the Santa Barbara channel coast. The Tsunami—moderate Geology Points value is estimated to be 1/10 that of Tsunami—high: 1/10 × $216 = $22.

For all other low-lying coastal areas the Tsunami—low factor applies. Its value is estimated to be 1/100 of Tsunami—high: 1/100 × 216 = 2.

Total tsunami damage loss to California, 1970 to 2000, if 1972 measures to reduce that loss continue unchanged, is estimated at $40,800,000. This figure is the sum of three elements: $15,700,000 losses to northern California facilities from tsunamis emanating from Alaskan earthquakes; $4,720,000 losses to southern California localities from tsunamis emanating from Chilean earthquakes; and $20,400,000 losses to Santa Barbara Channel shore localities if a catastrophic sea wave like that of 1812 (presumably caused by vertical movement on one of the active Channel faults) should be repeated.

Possible reduction of that 30-year loss, if all measures known and available in 1972 were to be rigorously applied, is estimated to be 95 percent, or $37,-760,000, mostly by zoning to exclude all vulnerable activities and structures from the areas accessible to tsunami waves, and tsunami-proofing those facilities that must remain.

Cost of those measures are estimated to be $25,700,-000, mostly one-time costs of indemnifying present owners of threatened property for its enforced reduced usefulness. The benefit:cost ratio would be about 1.5.

EVALUATION OF SUBSIDENCE LOSSES

Geology Points (Subsidence—high severity: 0.17;—low severity: 0.01) developed in Phase I of this study (California Division of Mines and Geology, 1971, p. 3-42 to 3-45) were doubled to account for the inherent intangible non-structural socio-economic factors. Life-loss and injury costs and disaster factor are both nil. Resulting Geology Points are:

Subsidence—high 0.34
Subsidence—low 0.02

Statewide, total damage, 1970–2000, assuming the 1972 type and level of loss reduction actions continues unchanged, is given in the table above.

Present-day subsidence-stabilization practices have proven to be relatively effective in preventing further subsidence loss in the state's principal subsidence-threat localities, Wilmington (Long Beach) oilfield, south San Francisco Bay margin in northern Santa Clara County; and California Water Project west-side aqueducts. Therefore most of the expected loss until 2000 will occur in other areas where subsidence is not yet perceived to be an urgent problem. An estimated 50 percent of the projected 30-year subsidence loss can be prevented by new, feasible programs; the total possible loss reduction, 1970–2000, is estimated to be $13,-180,000.

Costs of subsidence-abatement and prevention programs are almost impossible to isolate from the costs of concurrent programs intended to produce other benefits, without arbitrary cost apportionment.

For instance, about $80 million has been spent on water injection plants, wells, operating costs, and subsidence-monitoring costs in the subsiding part of the Wilmington (Long Beach) oil field from 1958 to 1971.

But the additional oil recovered by the repressuring and water-flooding action (estimated 80 percent of the 36,000 barrels per day recovered from this area in 1971 would not have been produced otherwise; Brock 1971, p. 13) has more than paid for all water-injection costs.

In another example, in Santa Clara County an extensive aquifer recharge program and the switching from underground to surface water supplies, has practically terminated subsidence. Both actions can be justified on the basis of water-supply economics alone. If it were important to charge a share of the costs of those programs against the subsidence-abatement benefit, 10–25 percent is estimated to be a reasonable share.

Practically, benefit:cost ratios of subsidence abatement programs range from about 1:1 where damage is repaired with few side benefits and the repair costs equal the damage costs (e.g., the 10-year program of repairing 90 miles of west-side aqueduct, at $141,000 per linear mile, or a total of $12,700,000—Golze, 1966), to localities like Long Beach and Santa Clara where an incalculable multiplier factor increases future land values by enabling high-value uses to proceed. Benefit:cost ratios of 100:1 and more are easily visualized, over extended time.

APPENDIX B

Population Projections*

A fundamental principle throughout the Urban Geology Master Plan is that priority for study of geologic hazards must be given to areas where the works of man will be built during the next 10 to 20 years. Although some large public works projects and extensive transportation and utility facilities are located outside urban areas, these usually are built after adequate geologic investigation. The major hazards to life and property are where people live (which, at the scale of this study, is also where they work). Critical development decisions in areas about to be urbanized or in the early stages of urban development are made by many individuals acting without sufficient knowledge of geologic hazards or of the increased hazard that will result from conversion of several thousand acres to urban use. Thus, the urban growth studies focus on areas that are not yet completely built up but will be experiencing rapid development in the near future.

* Slightly modified from Section 5, Phase I report (California Division of Mines and Geology, 1971).

CALIFORNIA URBAN GROWTH PROJECTIONS

The 1970 census data for counties, cities, and census county divisions were used to determine the present distribution of population throughout the state, and 1950 and 1960 census reports were analyzed to determine growth trends over the past two decades. The 1960 and 1970 census figures for all counties in California are shown on table 5. Growth projections made by Livingston and Blayney in April 1971, for each California county for 1980, 1990, and 2000 are also shown on table 5. These projections show the distribution of population if present development trends continue. The projections assume a year 2000 population of 33,900,000 for the state as projected by the California Department of Finance in its January, 1970, Provisional Population Projections. The Department's September, 1971, revised projection for 2000 is 32,267,000. These projections are lower than the California projections through 1985 prepared by the Bureau of the Census (Series II-B, Revised Projections of the Population of States, prepared in 1967), reflecting the impact of declining birth rates during the

Table 5. Regional population projections (condensed from table 6).

	1970		1990		1990	
	Census (in thousands)	Percent of state	Projection Livingston and Blayney (6/71) (in thousands)	Percent of state	Projection Department of Finance (9/71) (in thousands)	Percent of state
Los Angeles (5 counties)	9,971	50.0	14,820	51.1	13,802	49.5
San Diego (2 counties)	1,432	7.2	2,137	7.4	2,240	8.0
Northeast (8 counties)	294	1.5	388	1.3	363	1.3
North coast (5 counties)	194	1.0	212	0.7	245	0.9
San Francisco Bay area (9 counties)	4,628	23.2	6,572	22.7	6,507	23.4
Central coast (5 counties	762	3.8	1,266	4.4	1,182	4.2
North central (15 counties)	1,504	7.5	2,126	7.3	2,120	7.6
South central (9 counties)	1,168	5.9	1,479	5.1	1,430	5.1
Total state	19,953	100.0	29,000	100.0	27,888	100.0

Table 6. California population projections to the year 2000.

Region	Census 1960 (thousands)	Increase	Adv. Report 1970 (thousands)	Increase	1980 (thousands)	Increase	1990 (thousands)	Increase	2000 (thousands)	Dept. Finance 1990 (9/15/71)	Regional Agencies 1990 (thousands)	Source
LOS ANGELES												
Ventura	199	177	376	301	677	399	1,076	409	1,485	902,100	1,170	SCAG[3]
Los Angeles	6,039	993	7,032	869	7,901	952	8,853	917	9,770	8,663,700	9,400	SCAG
Orange	704	716	1,420	704	2,124	544	2,668	458	3,126	2,445,300	2,850	SCAG
San Bernardino	504	180	684	209	893	292	1,185	355	1,540	1,064,600	1,230	SCAG
Riverside	306	153	459	220	679	359	1,038	409	1,447	726,200	997	SCAG
Total	7,752	2,219	9,971	2,303	12,274	2,546	14,820	2,548	17,368	13,801,900	15,647	SCAG
%	49.3%	52.4%	50.0%	54.1%	50.7%	53.0%	51.1%	52.0%	51.2%	49.5%	—	
SAN DIEGO												
San Diego	1,033	325	1,358	313	1,671	366	2,037	378	2,415	2,141,500	2,350	S.D. Co. Plan
Imperial	72	2	74	9	83	17	100	15	115	98,100	101	SCAG
Total	1,105	327	1,432	323	1,755	382	2,137	393	2,530	2,239,600		
%	7.0%	7.7%	7.2%	7.6%	7.2%	8.0%	7.4%	8.0%	7.5%	8.0%		
NORTHEAST												
Siskiyou	33	0	33	1	34	1	35	2	37	36,300		
Modoc	8	-1	7	0	7	1	8	1	9	7,800		
Shasta	60	18	78	20	98	18	116	18	134	109,100		
Lassen	14	1	15	1	16	0	16	1	17	19,500		
Tehama	25	4	29	4	33	4	37	5	42	33,800		
Glenn	17	1	18	0	18	2	20	1	21	18,200		
Butte	82	20	102	21	123	19	142	19	161	125,400		
Plumas	12	0	12	0	12	2	14	2	16	13,100		
Total	251	43	294	47	341	47	388	49	437	363,200		
%	1.6%	1.0%	1.5%	1.1%	1.4%	1.0%	1.3%	1.0%	1.3%	1.3%		
NORTH COAST												
Del Norte	18	-3	15	-2	13	0	13	1	14	16,600		
Humboldt	105	-5	100	0	100	2	102	4	106	117,800		
Trinity	10	-2	8	-1	7	1	8	2	10	8,400		
Mendocino	51	0	51	5	56	6	62	8	70	68,800		
Lake	14	6	20	4	24	3	27	3	30	33,200		
Total	198	-4	194	6	200	12	212	18	230	244,800		
%	1.3%	—	1.0%	0.1%	8.2%	0.3%	0.7%	0.4%	0.7%	0.9%		
BAY AREA												
Sonoma	147	58	205	49	254	62	316	74	390	370,000	368	ABAG[4]/BATSC[5]
Napa	66	13	79	10	89	22	111	33	144	147,300	140	ABAG/BATSC
Solano	135	35	170	30	200	48	248	60	308	287,400	316	ABAG/BATSC
Marin	147	59	206	69	275	69	344	81	425	333,200	409	ABAG/BATSC
San Francisco	740	-24	716	80	696	15	711	14	725	716,300	827	ABAG/BATSC
San Mateo	444	112	556	116	672	122	804	111	915	676,800	873	ABAG/BATSC
Contra Costa	409	149	558	150	708	182	890	212	1,102	849,700	1,080	ABAG/BATSC
Alameda	908	165	1,073	149	1,222	180	1,402	182	1,584	1,368,400	1,681	ABAG/BATSC
Santa Clara	642	423	1,065	382	1,447	299	1,746	242	1,988	1,757,500	1,785	ABAG/BATSC
Total	3,638	990	4,628	935	5,563	1,009	6,572	1,009	7,581	6,506,600	7,477	ABAG/BATSC
%	23.2%	23.4%	23.2%	22.0%	22.9%	21.0%	22.7%	20.6%	22.4%	23.4%	—	
CENTRAL COAST												
Santa Cruz	84	40	124	38	162	43	205	40	245	208,600		
Monterey	198	52	250	60	310	75	385	74	459	340,400	340	Mont. County
San Benito	15	3	18	5	23	4	27	6	33	27,600		
San Luis Obispo	81	25	106	26	132	39	166	52	208	171,700		
Santa Barbara	169	95	264	100	364	119	483	102	585	433,600		
Total	547	215	762	229	991	275	1,266	274	1,530	1,181,900		
%	3.5%	5.1%	3.8%	5.4%	4.1%	5.7%	4.4%	5.6%	4.5%	4.2%		
NORTH CENTRAL												
Colusa	12	0	12	0	12	1	13	1	14	13,400		
Yolo	66	26	92	22	114	29	143	31	174	155,600	165	SRAPC[6]
Sutter	33	9	42	8	50	8	58	9	67	57,900	66	SRAPC
Yuba	34	11	45	8	53	9	62	12	74	51,900		
Sierra	2	0	2	0	2	1	3	1	4	2,700		
Nevada	21	5	26	5	31	5	36	6	42	37,200		
Placer	57	20	77	26	103	33	136	40	76	123,900	165	SRAPC
El Dorado	29	15	44	19	63	26	89	33	122	67,000	120	SRAPC
Amador	10	2	12	2	14	2	16	2	18	16,400		
Sacramento	503	128	631	117	748	120	868	122	990	852,100	1,010	SRAPC
San Joaquin	250	40	290	33	323	46	369	58	427	392,400		
Calaveras	10	4	14	3	17	4	21	5	26	20,300		
Stanislaus	157	38	195	35	230	45	275	54	329	292,400		
Tuolumne	15	7	22	7	29	7	36	8	44	36,400		
Alpine	0	0	0	0	0	1	1	0	1	700		
Total	1,199	305	1,504	285	1,789	337	2,126	382	2,508	2,120,300		
%	7.6%	7.2%	7.5%	6.7%	7.3%	7.0%	7.3%	7.8%	7.4%	7.6%		
SOUTH CENTRAL												
Merced	90	15	105	12	117	18	135	23	158	125,400		
Mariposa	5	1	6	2	8	2	10	3	13	9,900		
Madera	41	1	42	2	44	3	47	4	51	42,800		
Mono	2	2	4	0	4	1	5	1	6	9,100		
Fresno	366	47	413	49	462	75	537	93	630	503,900	850	(1)
Kings	50	15	65	6	71	12	83	14	97	74,100		
Tulare	169	19	188	17	205	30	235	40	275	236,400		
Inyo	12	4	16	0	16	1	17	1	18	24,600		
Kern	292	37	329	31	360	50	410	58	468	403,600	505	(2)
Total	1,027	141	1,168	119	1,287	192	1,479	237	1,716	1,429,800		
%	6.5%	3.3%	5.9%	2.8%	5.3%	4.0%	5.1%	4.8%	5.1%	5.1%		
STATE TOTAL (added)	15,717	4,236	19,953	4,247	24,200	4,800	29,000	4,900	33,900	27,888,100 100%		

(1) Grunwald 1985 extended to 1990
(2) Kern Co. Planning Commission 1985 extended to 1990
(3) Southern California Association of Governments
(4) Association of Bay Area Governments
(5) Bay Area Transportation Study Commission
(6) Sacramento Regional Area Planning Commission

last decade. Department of Finance unpublished projections[1] were analyzed for each county. Livingston and Blayney prepared projections for eight regional groupings of California counties for 1980, 1990, and 2000. The 1990 projections, shown on table 6, illustrate the differences between the Livingston and Blayney and the Department of Finance projections.

The regional differences are based on the following assumptions and judgments:

1. The greater Los Angeles metropolitan area (Los Angeles, Ventura, San Bernardino, Riverside, and Orange Counties) has the most diversified and resilient economy and will continue to grow faster than the state as a whole as long as expansion land is available without crossing major geographic barriers. Ventura, Riverside, and San Bernardino counties have vast amounts of contiguous undeveloped land.
2. San Diego County will increase its share of the state total slightly with a rate of growth about the same as that of the greater Los Angeles metropolitan area.
3. The San Francisco Bay area will decline slightly as a percentage of the state total in keeping with the trend in recent decades. Although the numerical growth will be substantial, the more rapid growth of southern California urban areas will reduce the San Francisco Bay area's share.
4. Despite substantial growth in the Sacramento metropolitan area, the 15-county North Central region will decline slightly as a percentage of the state for much the same reasons as the San Francisco Bay area.
5. The Central coast area (five counties) will increase its share on a small base (762,000—1970) because of available land and the high desirability of the coast. Santa Barbara, Monterey, and Santa Cruz counties were assigned substantially higher populations than the Department of Finance projections.
6. All other portions of California will have a declining percentage of the state because there will be little or no increase in employment in their agricultural, forest products, or tourist-oriented economies. Numerical growth will be modest, and in the North Coastal region, population is expected to remain nearly constant.

California's seven southernmost counties accounted for 62.4 percent of the state's population growth between 1950 and 1970, increasing from 52.5 percent of the state's total in 1950 to 57.2 percent in 1970. The projections assign 60.9 percent of the 1970–2000 increase to these counties, increasing their share of the state-wide population count to 58.7 percent by the end of the century. Barring unforeseen changes in employment patterns, southern California will continue to grow at a faster rate than the rest of the state. Projections for many of the counties are lower than locally prepared growth forecasts because recent experience shows these have been high and because the aggregate of locally prepared forecasts exceeds reasonable allocations of statewide projections to regions and counties within the state.

URBAN AREA DATA

Population forecasts and expected patterns of population distribution within counties and urban areas over the next three decades were developed by Livingston and Blayney after review of Department of Finance county projections, current plans, and projections of county and regional planning agencies, and judgments based on prior planning experience and knowledge of development trends in communities throughout the state. The projected distribution of population generally follows the expectations of local and regional planning agencies as to the directions of urban growth, although large open areas shown on some local plans are not assumed to remain open in the absence of implementation programs.

National forest lands and major military installations (notably Camp Pendleton) are assumed to be nondevelopable. Specific data sources for major urban regions are described below:

San Francisco Bay Region (Nine Counties)

County projections to 1990 and population distribution patterns projected by the Association of Bay Area Governments and the Bay Area Transportation Study Commission were examined. Data on vacant developable and nondevelopable lands within each county were studied. Population projections and land-use plans of the individual counties were reviewed. Major nondevelopable areas were delineated. By using county population projections by Livingston and Blayney, the probable pattern of growth was determined by allocating population to grid units on the basis of available land, existing trends, county and regional plans, and known development proposals.

Los Angeles Region (Five Counties)

Population projections for counties and subunits of counties compiled by the Southern California Association of Governments (SCAG) (Southern California Regional Development Guide report) from plans and projections of county and city planning agencies were analyzed. SCAG data on vacant developable and nondevelopable land and on existing population densities within the five counties also were reviewed. Major nondevelopable areas were mapped, and the projected population for each county prepared by Livingston and Blayney was allocated to grid units, taking account of local (county and SCAG) plans, current development trends, land availability, and major known development proposals.

San Diego County

County Planning Department projections of population for various planning areas within the county were reviewed, and county general-plan data were examined to ascertain likely directions of urban expansion. Location of major nondevelopable lands was determined, and projected population (Livingston and Blayney projections) was allocated to grid units based on community plans, current development trends, and land availability.

[1] Unofficial, unpublished projections for each county, prepared by the Department of Finance, were provided for analysis. These projections were made before complete 1970 census data were available and were adjusted September 15, 1971, after the Livingston and Blayney projections were completed. For six of the eight regional groupings, Livingston and Blayney projections are closer to the Department of Finance's September figures than to the Department's January provisional projections.

Sacramento-Stockton Urban Area (Six Counties)

Projections of 1990 population and distribution by the Sacramento Regional Area Planning Commission (SRAPC) for five counties and by San Joaquin County were examined. SRAPC projections made in 1968 are now believed by its staff to be too high, and Livingston and Blayney projections for the region are lower. The projected population was allocated to grid units within the urban portions of the six counties based on present patterns, known development proposals, and probable development trends indicated by available planning studies.

Fresno and Kern Counties

Projected Fresno County population was assigned to grid units, primarily following present patterns of growth. Principal sources of data were the 1985 County General Plan, and recent population and growth alternative studies reported by the Central Fresno County Water and Liquid Waste Study, Volume II.

Kern County projections were provided by the county planning department, but these were admittedly too high. Lower projections by Livingston and Blayney were used to estimate future growth patterns in the Bakersfield urban area grid units.

Santa Cruz and Monterey Counties

The amount of developable land in Santa Cruz and northern Monterey counties was determined, and Livingston and Blayney projections of county population were distributed to grid units following the general growth patterns anticipated by the planning department of each county.

URBAN DEVELOPMENT DATA PRESENTATION

In order to reduce the distribution of population into manageable data units comparable with units for which geologic factors also could be measured and tabulated, a uniform "grid" system made up of USGS 7½-minute quad sheets divided into four quadrants of about 15 square miles each was selected. This grid was applied to all portions of the state which now are urbanized and which might be expected to become urbanized during the next 30 years. The U.S. Census definition of Standard Metropolitan Statistical Area (SMSA) was used as the criterion for selection of areas to be mapped with this grid. Thus, all areas expected to have a central city of 50,000 or more by 2000 are covered. Figures 14 through 20, Urban Growth Projections, at 1:250,000, show the areas mapped. Developable (urbanized) square miles in each grid were estimated using available local studies and a definition of land over 25–30 percent slope as undevelopable. By this means, a gross measurement of the land area available for urban development was obtained.

Examination of densities of development in the San Francisco Bay area and southern California indicated that when the gross population density of an urban area exceeds about 5,000 persons per square mile of developed urban land (including all nonresidential uses) the area can be considered to be at full development with little space remaining for added development unless rebuilding occurs at greater intensity, as in city cores. Typical urban development characterized by the extensive portions of the San Fernando Valley and the Santa Clara Valley that have been urbanized in the last 25 years has a gross density of about 4,000 persons per square mile. While about half of the state's population resides or works in areas already fully developed, these offer the least opportunity for new or corrective measures to reduce or eliminate geological hazards and minimize damage. The greatest benefits of the study will be in areas yet to be developed or areas not yet completely built up. The lowest priority for study would be in areas that are not expecred to see significant development during the next 30 years. Accordingly, it was determined that a threshold definition of "urban" as 1,000 persons per developable square mile would be used because it indicates commitment of land to urban use, and is used by the U. S. Census. In most instances, an average existing density of 1,000 persons per square mile does not result from very large lots or widely scattered development. Rather, it usually indicates that 20 to 25 percent of a grid is developed at the typical urban fringe densities of 4,000 to 5,000 persons per square mile achieved where single-family houses are the dominant building type.

Population projections for counties were allocated to each grid unit on the basis of present (1970 census) population, developable square miles, and probable development patterns assuming no major governmental intervention that would alter present trends. The 1970 census data for census county divisions and incorporated cities were used, and 1980, 1990, and 2000 population within counties was allocated on the basis of local plans and a "trends" assumption that continued the present growth pattern. Inability to predict the sequence of development within adjoining grids and the necessarily rough estimate of the area of developable land require that the individual grid projections be viewed as rough approximations. However, there can be a higher level of confidence in the projections for groups of grids surrounding an existing urban area.

Nearly all areas of concentrated employment are close to urban-density residential areas. Looking at 15-square-mile grids, the residential population is the controlling factor, because grids that have 15,000 or more jobs also have 15,000 or more residents. A refinement not possible within the scope of this study (or necessary, in our opinion) would be to add daytime and nighttime populations in each grid.

A set of five maps covering all existing and potential SMSA's by the year 2000 has been prepared and color-coded to show whether each grid unit is currently "fully developed" (over 5,000 persons per square mile), is currently urban (developed at over 1,000 persons per square mile but with potential for added population growth), or will become urban by 1980, 1990, or 2000. Major lands that are nondevelopable or that will not be developed by 2000 are also shown. These maps have a scale of 1:250,000 and are reproduced on figures 14 through 20, "Projected Population Distribution and Density." A second set of maps at the 1:250,000 scale with notations in each grid showing developable square miles, population density in 1970, 1980, 1990, and 2000 were completed and are held as office maps by the Division of Mines and Geology at their Headquarters Office, Sacramento.

A 1:1,000,000 scale map of the state (California Division of Mines and Geology, 1971, figure 5-1) shows the locations of areas covered by the detailed grid maps. This figure also shows the location of communities having 5,000 or more population in 1970 that are not located in areas classified as urban by the 1,000-persons-per-square-mile definition or in areas covered by the grid maps. Communities projected to reach 5,000 in 1980, 1990, and 2000 were not located, because the inability to project small-area growth with sufficient accuracy, and the small exposure to hazards in comparison with larger urban areas, surely would result in a low priority for study.

The total area covered by the grids contains a 1970 population of 18,881,000 representing 95 percent of the state's 19,953,000 residents. The same area by 2000 is expected to house 32,247,000 persons, holding at 95 percent of the state total.

CONCLUSIONS

The growth analysis indicates that population growth will occur mainly on the fringes of present urban areas, for the most part in areas already recognized for their growth potential and "in the path" of outwardly spreading subdivision activity. Extensive new urban development outside the present metropolitan areas will not be required to accommodate the projected state population, and large new towns or accelerated growth of small freestanding communities will result only if public policy actively restrains and redirects growth of present urban areas. There are no signs that such policies will be adopted in the near future. No attempt has been made to predict the location of new towns in non-urbanizing regions. Neither was any significant population allocated to the many recreational and wilderness-oriented subdivisions that are being promoted throughout the state.

The trends projection shows that by 2000 southern California urbanization will cover virtually all the developable portions of Ventura and Orange Counties, and will be occurring in the Palmdale-Lancaster portion of the Mojave Desert. Urbanization of the San Bernardino-Riverside area will, by then, have merged fully with the easterly spread of the Los Angeles area, and the new fringe of the metropolitan region will be reaching San Gorgonio Pass and into the northwestern portion of the Perris Valley. Most of western San Diego County from the Mexican border north to Camp Pendleton and Fallbrook will fall within the urban definition by 2000. Virtually all the coastal shelf adjoining Santa Barbara will be urbanized. Between San Luis Obispo and San Diego, urbanization will occupy about twice the land area now defined as urban, but much of the area will be only partially developed.

San Francisco Bay Region growth also is expected to follow predictable courses, with the spread of continuous urban area northward into southern Sonoma County, easterly to Antioch and Livermore areas, and south through the Santa Clara Valley to Gilroy. Other growth areas will be the Santa Cruz-Watsonville and the Monterey-Salinas areas on Monterey Bay, and southern Solano County.

In the Sacramento and San Joaquin Valleys, the expecred pattern of expansion will enlarge existing urban areas, but fusion of presently identifiable, discrete urban areas into continuous urban strips is not expected. The largest single metropolitan area in the Central Valley will be the Sacramento-Roseville-Folsom area.

Outside the areas covered by the grid maps, only Eureka, South Lake Tahoe, Madera, and El Centro have populations large enough to approximate urban areas within the gridded areas, but none is expected to contain a central city of 50,000 by 2000.

If added urban development were to be the sole criterion for study priority, and the areas that will reach urban density by 1980 were rated most crucial, first priority study areas would include Ventura County, Orange County, and the Ontario-San Bernardino-Riverside area of southern California, and the San Francisco Bay area's southern Santa Clara Valley.

APPENDIX C
Summary of Significant Court Decisions and Legislation

In recent years there have been many attempts by government to reduce losses from geologic hazards. The following summaries are some of the more important ones.

COURT DECISIONS

1. Sheffet decision (Los Angeles Superior Court Case No. 32487): Declared that a public entity is liable for damages to adjacent property resulting from improvements planned, specified or authorized by the public entity in the exercise of its governmental power. (The State Supreme Court refused to rehear this decision, which establishes a judicial precedent.)

2. L. A. County Superior Court (Case No. 684595 and consolidated cases): This decision found the County liable for damages which may have resulted from roadwork and the placement of fill by the County. This case was in regard to the Portuguese Bend landslide, Palos Verdes Hills, Los Angeles County, California.

3. City of Bakersfield vs. Miller (48 Cal. Rptr. 889), heard in the State Supreme Court 1966: This decision affirms that the city may declare an older structure not in compliance with the newly adopted Uniform Building Code to be a public nuisance. Further the city may enforce abatement of the nonconforming condition even though to do so may require the building to be demolished.
4. Burgess vs. Conejo Valley Development Co. (Connor vs. Great Western Savings and Loan Association) (73 Cal. Rptr. 369) heard in the State Supreme Court in 1968, concerning damage to tract homes from expansive soil in Thousand Oaks, Ventura County: This decision affirmed that the home buyer, both first buyer and all subsequent ones, has the right to protection from negligent construction practice leading to damage. In this case, neither contractor, county inspectors, nor representatives of the major lending institution acted to ascertain expansive soil conditions, or to prevent damage from them.
5. Oakes vs. The McCarthy Co. (California Appellate Reports, 2d Series, 267, 1968) the court held that in the Palos Verdes area, Los Angeles County, a developer and soils engineering company could be liable in negligence for damages to a home resulting from using improper (clay) fill material and improperly compacting that fill so that earth movement resulted. Also, the court awarded punitive damages against the developer for fraudulent concealment of material facts concerning the property, i.e., failure to volunteer to the prospective buyer that the house was built upon fill.

LEGISLATION

Public Resources Code

Section 660–662 and 2621–2625: These sections require the State Geologist to delineate special studies zones encompassing potentially and recently active fault traces. It requires cities and counties to exercise specified approval authority with respect to real estate developments or structures for human occupancy within such delineated zones.

Section 2700–2708: These sections require the Division of Mines and Geology to purchase and install strong-motion instruments (to measure the effects of future earthquakes) in representative structure and geologic environments throughout the state.

Section 2750: Establishes a state mining and minerals policy which, among other things, encourages wise use of mineral resources.

Education Code

Section 15002.1: This section requires that geological and soils engineering studies be conducted on all new school sites and on existing sites where deemed necessary by the Department of General Services.

Section 15451–15466: These sections constitute the Field Act and require that public schools be designed for the protection of life and property. These sections, enacted in 1933 after the Long Beach earthquake, are enforced by the State Office of Architecture and Construction in accordance with regulations contained in Title 21 of the California Administrative Code.

Health and Safety Code

Sections 15000 et seq.: These sections require that geological and engineering studies be conducted on each new hospital or additions affecting the structure of an existing hospital, excepting therefrom one story Type V buildings 4000 sq. ft. or less in area.

Sections 19100–19150: These sections constitute the Riley Act and require certain buildings to be constructed to resist lateral forces, specified in Title 24 California Administrative Code.

Section 17922, 17951–17958.7: These sections require cities and counties to adopt and enforce the Uniform Building Code, including a grading section (chap. 70), a minimum protection against some geologic hazards.

Business and Professions Code

Section 7800–7887: These sections provide for the registration of geologists and geophysicists, and the certification of certain geologists in the specialty of engineering geology.

Section 11010: This section requires that a statement of the soil conditions be prepared and needed modifications be carried out in accordance with the recommendations of a registered civil engineer.

Section 11100–11629: These sections require studies in subdivisions to evaluate the possibilities of flooding and unfavorable soils.

Government Code

Section 8589.5: This section requires that inundation maps and emergency evacuation plans be completed for areas subject to inundation by dam failure.

Section 65300–65302.1: These sections require that each city and county shall adopt the following elements:

- Seismic safety element consisting of the identification and appraisal of seismic hazards including an appraisal of landsliding due to seismic events.
- Conservation element including the conservation, development and utilization of minerals.
- Safety element including protection of the community from geologic hazards including mapping of known geologic hazards.

INDEX

(Numbers in italic are pages that have illustrations; numbers in parentheses immediately following entry indicate section of this report.)

84769—650 8/73 3M 25X

CPSIA information can be obtained
at www.ICGtesting.com
Printed in the USA
BVHW081010200219
540731BV00027B/1712/P

9 780282 281830